SITTING BULL

AND OTHER LEGENDARY
NATIVE AMERICAN CHIEFS

SITTING BULL

AND OTHER LEGENDARY
NATIVE AMERICAN CHIEFS

✦ ✦ ✦ ✦ ✦ **BREE BURNS** ✦ ✦ ✦ ✦ ✦

CRESCENT BOOKS

NEW YORK • AVENEL, NEW JERSEY

A FRIEDMAN GROUP BOOK

This 1993 edition published by Crescent Books, distributed by Outlet Book Company, Inc., a Random House Company, 40 Engelhard Avenue, Avenel, New Jersey 07001.

Random House
New York • Toronto • London • Sydney • Auckland

ISBN 0-517-07344-7

SITTING BULL
And Other Legendary Native American Chiefs
was prepared and produced by
Michael Friedman Publishing Group, Inc.
15 West 26th Street
New York, New York 10010

Editor: Kelly Matthews
Art Director: Jeff Batzli
Designers: Robert W. Kosturko and Lynne Yeamans
Photography Editor: Ede Rothaus

Printed in Hong Kong and bound in China by Leefung-Asco Printers Ltd.

8 7 6 5 4 3 2 1

DEDICATION

For John and Dorothy Burns

ACKNOWLEDGMENTS

The author wishes to thank the following: Priscilla Burns; Constance Jones and Heather Lewis; Jill Kirschen; Mark Ameen; Neil Greenberg; Elizabeth Ilgenfritz; Ellen Scordato; Betsy Wilcox; Ruth and Arthur Vogel; Kym and Ariel Moore; the Library of the Department of Indian Affairs, Ottawa, Canada; the Royal British Columbia Museum; the Alaska State Museum; the New York Public Library; and Kelly Matthews at the Michael Friedman Publishing Group.

·TABLE OF CONTENTS·

INTRODUCTION ✳ 9

CHAPTER ONE ✳ THE LEGEND OF HIAWATHA ✳ 10

CHAPTER TWO ✳ KING PHILIP, LEADER OF THE WAMPANOAG ✳ 16

CHAPTER THREE ✳ POPÉ AND THE PUEBLO REVOLT ✳ 24

CHAPTER FOUR ✳ PONTIAC'S WAR IN THE WILDERNESS ✳ 30

CHAPTER FIVE ✳ MAQUINNA OF VANCOUVER ISLAND ✳ 36

CHAPTER SIX ✳ TECUMSEH, THE GREATEST HOPE ✳ 46

CHAPTER SEVEN ✳ OSCEOLA, ALABAMA-BORN SEMINOLE CHIEF ✳ 52

CHAPTER EIGHT ✳ RIVAL CHIEFS BLACK HAWK AND KEOKUK ✳ 58

CHAPTER NINE ✳ LAKOTA CHIEF SITTING BULL ✳ 64

CHAPTER TEN ✳ CRAZY HORSE, "A GOOD DAY TO DIE" ✳ 74

CHAPTER ELEVEN ✳ CHIEF JOSEPH AND THE NEZ PERCE RETREAT ✳ 84

CHAPTER TWELVE ✳ GERONIMO ✳ 92

EPILOGUE ✳ TWENTIETH-CENTURY CHIEFS ✳ 100

APPENDIX A ✳ NATIVE AMERICAN ORGANIZATIONS ✳ 103

APPENDIX B ✳ NATIVE AMERICAN MUSEUMS ✳ 105

BIBLIOGRAPHY ✳ 109

INDEX ✳ 111

From the Iroquois nation of the northeastern United States to the Pueblo peoples of the Southwest, the natives of North America, although not a homogeneous people, do have one common bond: they have all shared the same challenges to their freedom, personal security, means of existence, and life itself since the Europeans arrived on the North American continent. Legendary chiefs rose from different tribes to confront the crisis; some were military leaders, some were spiritual leaders, and most were both. Their names—Pontiac, Tecumseh, Sitting Bull, Crazy Horse, Geronimo, and others—may be familiar, but the details of their struggles, triumphs, and defeats are largely unknown to most people.

The leaders included in *Sitting Bull and Other Legendary Native American Chiefs* were selected to provide an overview of a variety of Native American tribes from across the continent. Arranged chronologically, the twelve chiefs that are included here only touch the surface of the rich and fascinating history of the natives of North America, so once your interest has been sparked, be sure to read more about their lives, traditions, and culture.

The Legend of Hiawatha

SONGS OF THE CORN DANCE

Among the flowers I am moving reverently.
Among the flowers I am singing, dancing.
Berries ripen,
Fruit ripens.

—SENECA SONG OF THANKSGIVING

HIAWATHA WAS BORN EITHER A MOHAWK or an Onondaga in present-day upstate New York. Little is known about his early years. According to legend, Hiawatha married the daughter of a chief, had from three to seven daughters, and became an influential medicine man or magician noted for his oratorial powers. By the time he became well known in the latter half of the sixteenth century, Iroquois tribes were at constant war with each other. Hiawatha helped to organize five separate, savagely hostile Iroquoian tribes, who were among the most intellectually advanced groups of Indians north of Mexico, into a very advanced political league—unified by a system of law—known as the Five Nations, initiating a long period of calm among them known as "the Great Peace." The story of Hiawatha has come down to the present day in mythological form—of which there are many versions—designed to teach the important principles of peace and brotherhood. The real Hiawatha was not the fictionalized Chippewa hero of Henry Wadsworth Longfellow's poem.

Spread throughout the Appalachian forests of the eastern part of North America were two

great divisions of Iroquoian-speaking people who were still ignorant of European invaders. The Northern tribes included Hurons, Eries, Honnaisonts, Conestogas, and Susquehannocks in Pennsylvania and Ohio. Five closely related tribes that called themselves Haudenasaunee, or "people of the extended lodge," lived in the lake and river valleys between present-day Albany and Buffalo in New York. These tribes included the Senecas, Cayugas, Onondaga, Oneidas, and Mohawks. They fought over fishing and hunting rights and engaged in the custom of blood revenge: Every time a man was killed, his slaying had to be avenged; a member of his tribe would murder the man who had killed him. The result was endless warfare and anarchy among tribes.

LEFT: Hiawatha spread the message of unification among the Five Tribes of the Iroquois.

ABOVE: Hiawatha's legacy survives through the dramatization of a myth in which Hiawatha banishes the evil that caused the fighting between tribes and teaches a philosophy based on righteousness, health, and power.

RIGHT: A fragment of a sixteenth-century wampum belt survives as a symbol of the unity of the Iroquois Nation. Purple and white beads made from whelk shells form squares that represent the nations of the Iroquois League, united by the chain of friendship.

But there were also leaders who remembered the teachings of Teharonhiawagon, the Master of Life, the first being on earth, who commanded men to love each other and live in peace. In Iroquoian mythology, he was opposed by an evil brother who led the Indians in wrongdoings, but Teharonhiawagon had promised to send a messiah to the tribes to help them fight evil when their need became great. Iroquoian leaders, including Hiawatha, began to look for this messiah and proposed a council of leaders to discuss the future of their people.

There was, however, a fierce and clever Onondaga chief named Atotarho who opposed Hiawatha and the council of reformers. In his legendary guise, Atotarho is fiendish, possibly the Master of Life's evil brother. His body is described as being distorted by seven crooks, his hands appear as those of a turtle, and his hair is a mass of writhing snakes. He was a terrible tyrant, hated and feared by the Iroquoian people. Atotarho directed his venom at Hiawatha by killing the latter's daughters. Despite these attacks on his family, Hiawatha continued to organize the council. The murder of Hiawatha's last daughter was cunningly undertaken. Atotarho pointed to the sky and shouted, "Look up! Something living is falling. What is it?" The people looked up and saw a beautiful creature plummeting through the sky toward the forest where Hiawatha's daughter was gathering wood. In a great rush, they ran to the forest and, in their frenzy, trampled Hiawatha's daughter to death. Hiawatha, grief-stricken, decided to leave the Onondagas and carry his message to other Iroquoian tribes.

In this version of the Hiawatha myth, he wandered from village to village, pleading with the leaders of the Mohawks, Oneidas, and Cayugas to renounce war and murder and restore peace and brother-

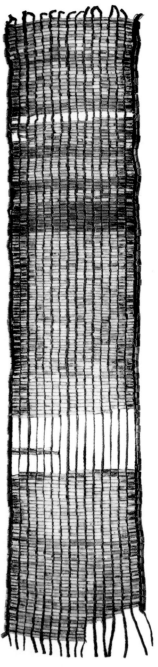

hood among the Iroquois. Eventually all the tribes agreed, but only under the condition that Hiawatha persuade Atotarho to end his evil ways and bring the Onondagas into peaceful relations with the rest of the tribes.

At this point, Deganawidah, a supernatural being who is known as the "Peacemaker" by the Iroquois and was born of a virgin birth and sent to bring peace to the world, entered Hiawatha's life. Deganawidah had already heard of Hiawatha but was distressed when he heard that he was a cannibal. (While it is possible that the Iroquois were actually cannibals, it is also likely that this aspect of the myth served to represent the violent aspect of their culture.) Going to Hiawatha's lodge and finding him away, Deganawidah climbed to the roof and lay flat on his stomach, looking down through the smoke hole. Hiawatha returned with the dead body of an Indian, which he cut up and cooked. As he

reached into the kettle to pull out the cooked flesh, he saw the face of Deganawidah reflected in the water and mistook it for his own. Concluding that so beautiful a face did not agree with the hideousness of cannibalism, he decided to give it up. As he went outside to empty the kettle, he met Deganawidah and confessed to him what had occurred. Deganawidah congratulated him on his decision and enlisted him in his peace mission.

To Hiawatha's appeals for an end to intertribal warring, Deganawidah contributed a plan of unified government based upon a set of principles, or laws. But because Deganawidah stuttered, Hiawatha became the messenger to the tribes. One by one, each of the Five Nations agreed and accepted what was to become known as the Great Peace. Again, however, it was Atotarho and the Onondagas who remained the final stumbling block.

Deganawidah, Hiawatha, and the other chiefs visited Atotarho together. To aid them in straightening out Atotarho's twisted mind and body, they made thirteen strings of wampum and sang the Six Songs, which were part of the rites of the Dead Feast. As they unwrapped the wampum and began to sing the Six Songs, Atotarho became entranced. Deganawidah said, "This song hereafter shall belong to you alone. It is called 'I use it to beautify the earth.'" As Atotarho's mind began to change, Deganawidah transformed his feet into those of a normal man. He restored Atotarho's deformed hands and brushed the snakes from his hair saying, "Your head shall now be like that of a human being." Other versions of the story have Hiawatha combing the serpents out of Atotarho's hair (Hiawatha's name means literally "he, the comber"). Finally, Deganawidah straightened Atotarho's twisted body and the evil chief was redeemed.

The clan leaders were then able to gather around their fires to fashion the laws of their government and new federation under the guidance of Deganawidah and Hiawatha. To the new council, which could be called into session whenever necessary but was obliged to meet every five years, would be sent fifty *sachems,* or chiefs, appointed by the female leaders of tribal *ohwachiras*, the Iroquoian matrilineal family units. The first of Deganadiwah's three basic principles outlawed cannibalism, except as a symbolic act during war against enemies of the Great Peace (eating an enemy's heart was said to give the consumer the dead warrior's courage and skills). The second guaranteed the rights of individuals to safety and justice. The final and most important reform ended the custom of the blood feud.

LEFT: An area that served as the Senecas' ancient hunting grounds is located in present-day Allegheny State Park, which is located in western New York State. Some members of the Seneca tribe live on a nearby reservation.

RIGHT: Some members of the Iroquois tribe traveled abroad, such as Tee Yee Neen Ho Ga Row, a Mohawk sachem who was said to have visited Queen Anne in 1610. Friendly with the British, the Iroquois voted to join forces with them during the American Revolution. The Oneidas and the Tuscaroras disagreed with the decision and broke off from the League, the Oneidas fighting on the colonists' side and the Tuscaroras remaining neutral. The nations have never been as powerful individually as they were when they were united.

Deganawidah entered a canoe of luminous white stone and disappeared forever. Hiawatha remained behind and became an apostle and missionary, carrying the council's message far and wide to other Iroquoian tribes, but his successes were few. Ironically, war parties fought fanatically against peoples who resisted the league. By the time Hiawatha died, he was accepted as a man who had been close to the Master of Life. Soon after his death, his name became shrouded in mystery and legend. Through two strife-torn centuries, the unity of Hiawatha's confederation maintained the power and strength of the Five Nations. And the principles at the heart of the Iroquois system of government have been included among the studies of European and American philosophers who were seeking more just and humane ways for humankind to govern itself.

DEGANAWIDAH, THE PEACEMAKER

A fter his death, the Peacemaker, Deganawidah, who came to guide and direct Hiawatha, was elevated to the status of a demigod. Most people today believe he was a real man, but his story has come down through the ages as more of a legend.

Deganawidah came from the land of the Hurons, the Iroquoian "crooked tongues" who lived along the lakes in eastern Ontario. He was said to be the son of an unmarried virgin, though this might reflect Christian influences sown later among the Iroquois. His mother, Djigosasee, lived alone with her mother on the outskirts of a village. She was too poor and despised to belong to a clan. Her mother was furious about Djigosasee's pregnancy until one night she dreamed that her daughter was telling the truth about being a virgin. The dream told her that a male child would be born whom they should name Deganawidah, meaning "the thinker," and that he would indirectly be the cause of the ruin of the Huron people.

Because they considered the child's destiny to be evil, the women decided to kill Deganawidah after his birth. They took the newborn to a frozen stream and dropped him through a hole in the ice. When they awoke the next morning, the baby was sleeping unharmed between them. They tried to kill him two more times but were unsuccessful. They finally decided that it was the will of the Master of Life that they raise the child.

Deganawidah grew into manhood ignored and persecuted by the other Hurons. His mother was his only companion, and she taught him tolerance and love, telling him that he had been given a divine mission. He was lonely and stammered severely but had a handsome face that reflected his mystic soul.

One day Deganawidah had a powerful vision. He saw a great spruce tree growing toward the sky in soil composed of three double principles of life. Those principles were sanity of mind and body/peace between individuals and groups; righteousness in conduct, thought, and speech/equity and justice among peoples; and physical strength and civil authority/power of the *orenda*. (Orenda was the inner spiritual power that helped the Indians resist malevolent forces. One man's orenda was small, but it contributed to the combined, greater orenda of firesides, ohwachiras, and clans.) The tree was anchored in the ground by five roots; from its base stretched a snow-white carpet that covered the countryside. On top of the tree was an eagle. In the symbolism of his vision, Deganawidah recognized the tree as humanity, growing from the basic principles of virtuous relations among men. The soil protected the lands of the tribes that adopted the three double principles, but it could be extended to the ends of the earth to provide the shelter of brotherhood and peace to every nation and race of mankind. The five roots were the five Iroquoian tribes that gave the tree its support; the eagle was humanity's lookout against any enemies that might try to disturb the peace. Deganawidah now understood his mission. After saying good-bye to his mother, he left the country of the crooked tongues and traveled to other Iroquoian lands, looking for disciples and converts.

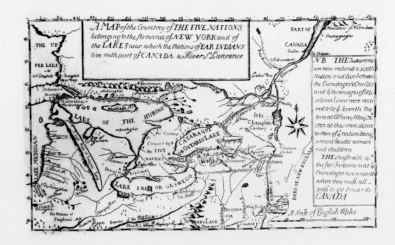

LEFT: In 1712, the powerful confederation of the League of Iroquois Nations grew to include the Tuscarora tribe. Each nation was allotted a certain number of votes, except the Tuscaroras, who, being latecomers, were not allowed to vote. Representatives to the general council meetings were chosen by women, who instructed the men how to vote. If the men did not follow their instructions, the women could remove them from the council.

ABOVE: The Great Peace spread over large portions of present-day upstate New York, an area that includes the Genesee River. By the end of the seventeenth century, the Five Nations controlled the area from the Ottawa River south to the Cumberland River in Tennessee and westward from Maine to Lake Michigan.

CHAPTER TWO

King Philip, Leader of the Wampanoag

Welcome, Englishmen. Welcome, Englishmen.

—SAMOSET TO THE PLYMOUTH COLONISTS,
MARCH 1621

KING PHILIP WAS THE SON OF MASSASOIT, THE Wampanoag chief who established a friendly alliance with the Pilgrims of Plymouth colony in present-day Massachusetts. Unlike his father, however, King Philip felt that the colonists were enemies who would have to be stopped. Philip was heir to peaceful surface relations between the colonists and natives, but his heritage also included the knowledge of white injustices and the still-festering wounds they had caused in the hearts of many Indians, who had as yet made no outcry against them. These injustices included the kidnapping of twenty-four Indians from the New England coast by explorer Thomas Hunt in 1614, who took them to Màlaga to sell as slaves. To the Puritans of New England, Philip was simply "a hell-hound, fiend, serpent, caitiff, and dog" who led a conspiracy and uprising against their established authority. Ironically, betrayal and disunity on Philip's side became the bitter theme of his war against the colonists, which lasted from 1675 to 1676.

Before his death, Massasoit asked the General Court at Plymouth to give English names to his two older sons, Wamsutta and

Metacom. Being reminded of the two kings at Macedon, the English named them Alexander and Philip, and on Massasoit's death, Alexander succeeded to the chieftainship of the Wampanoags. By then, a new generation of colonists had replaced the grateful Pilgrims. These colonists were claiming more and more Wampanoag land and persecuting non-Christianized Indians, who were deemed guilty of blasphemy.

Alexander was summoned before the Plymouth authorities to assure them of his loyalty. During the interrogation, he became ill with fever. He died on the trip back to his village. The Indians were enraged, believing that Alexander had died of bitterness over his rude treatment or that he had been poisoned by the white men. During this crisis, Philip donned the wampum mark of chieftainship at Mount Hope. He was twenty-four years old and hot-tempered, quick to respond to an affront. Once, an Indian who was friendly to the English had insulted the name of the dead Massasoit, and in a rage, Philip pursued him across forty miles of water to Nantucket. Philip was convinced that the colonists had killed Alexander and was determined to avenge his brother's death.

For thirteen years, Philip kept the settlers on edge, alternately living at peace with them and suddenly threatening to prepare for war against the New England townspeople. Philip sent runners through the woods on diplomatic journeys to other tribes, attempting to unite them against the colonists. Many chiefs were suspicious, but Philip eventually gained support from the two largest tribes in southern New England: the Narragansets (traditional enemies of the Wampanoag), who lived west of the bay in Rhode Island that bears their name, and the Nipmucks, whose members were spread across the interior forests of Massachusetts. He was unable, however, to convince the Niantics of the western Rhode Island shorefront and the Mohegans and Pequots of Connecticut as well as the Massachusetts natives of the north who were

LEFT: King Philip surprised his English enemies by abundantly arming his warriors with muskets. The Indians had made progress in gunsmithing; Indian forges in the forests became primary military objectives for the colonists.

ABOVE RIGHT: The noble Massasoit, as he was formally addressed, invited the Pilgrims to their first Thanksgiving dinner and remained friendly with the colonists despite their repeated usurpations of Wampanoag land. The chief's Indian name was Wasamegin, meaning "Yellow Feather."

all deeply involved with the whites and were certain they were too strong to defeat. Even the Sakonnets, a branch of Wampanoag who lived south of Mount Hope and were ruled by a squaw sachem named Awashonks, avoided promising their support.

The war that finally did come was precipitated by treachery. In January 1675, John Sassamon, a Christianized Indian who was Philip's secretary, paid a visit to the Plymouth governor and told him everything that Philip was planning. When Sassamon was later found dead, the authorities believed it was on Philip's orders and rounded up three Wampanoags for the murder. When the Indians were found guilty by the white court and hanged, the tribe exploded in anger.

Almost at once, reports reached Plymouth that a crisis was in the making. A settler named Benjamin Church, who had acquired land from the Sakonnets and had become friendly with their squaw sachem, Awashonks, attended a native dance at her village and found six people from Philip's tribe present. They were painted for war, and shot bags and rattlesnake skins were hung down their backs. Awashonks, who was fond of Church, informed him that Philip was urging her to join in a war against the English. Soon after, Church rode into Plymouth to tell the authorities of Philip's plans.

On June 20, 1675, an angry group of Wampanoags—whose actions were probably not sanctioned by Philip—came into Swansea, shot some cattle, and ransacked the village. The English retaliated a few days later. Soon the Wampanoag were swarming out of Mount Hope, stripped and painted for war. They shot and killed nine settlers as they came along the roads or went into their fields.

As the hostilities escalated, Philip and his tribe, now joined by Alexander's wife, Wetamoo, and the Pocasset tribe, found themselves in an all-out war. They struck savagely at nearby settlements, burning the towns of Rehoboth, Taunton, Dartmouth, and Middleborough. Panic spread across New England. Some Christianized natives, or "praying Indians" as they were called, and a well-armed band of Mohegans from Connecticut agreed to join the colonists, hoping to get some Wampanoag scalps and booty. Philip, however, also gained some important allies, the Nipmucks, who were encouraged by the Wampanoags'

initial success. These newcomers were led by their own war chiefs, including old Matoonas, Monoco (also known as "One-Eyed John"), Shoshanim (whom the whites called "Sagamore Sam"), and a warrior by the name of Mattaump. The Nipmucks regarded Philip as the symbol of their cause and the bloodshed soon spread throughout the Connecticut River Valley.

Philip then gained the alliance of the Narragansets, who had initially resisted joining the conflict. They gave Weetamoo's people sanctuary after they fled from Pocasset country with Philip. This angered the colonists, who forced Canonchet, the Narraganset leader, to sign an agreement promising to surrender Weetamoo within ten days. When the time limit passed, they sent their troops into the Narraganset fort.

The Indians met the English with a burst of gunfire and drove them back. But by the time the conflict ended, more than six hundred Indian men, women, and children had died, "terribly Barbikew'd,"

ABOVE: Discovered in 1912, this stone pipe depicting a bear figure holding onto a bowl reportedly belonged to King Philip.

LEFT: One of the most dramatic battles of King Philip's War was fought on an island on the west side of Narragansett Bay known as the Great Swamp. On December 19, 1675, the colonists pushed across the icy surface of the wild marsh, coming upon a fort that held more than three thousand Indians. The two sides fought hand-to-hand for hours, with the settlers finally setting fire to the Indians' settlement. The surviving Indians disappeared into the dark and frozen swamp.

RIGHT: The rolling hills and quiet lakes of the New England countryside were the site of the most devastating war the area has ever experienced.

according to a later account by the Boston preacher Cotton Mather. Canonchet, Weetamoo, and others managed to escape, and the settlers, who had suffered casualties of their own, withdrew through a dark and frozen marsh.

In dozens of camps, war bands of Indians were waiting to strike again. Under Philip's orders, they were to burn villages and kill people until all the whites were dead or driven from the country. Soon the Indians were conducting devastating raids on the English colonies in Massachusetts, Rhode Island, and Connecticut. Out of ninety white settlements, fifty-two had been attacked and twelve were destroyed.

The Indians' momentum slowed as doubts, fear, and treachery set in. Large groups of Indians who knew how to fight in the woods and swamps as effectively as Philip's men joined the colonists. Some Connecticut volunteers and Indian auxiliaries tracked and captured Canonchet. Before he was shot by a Pequot, Canonchet announced, "I shall die before my heart is soft, or I have said anything unworthy of myself." His corpse was quartered and burned by representatives of the Mohegans, Niantics, and Pequots. His head was sent to the authorities at Hartford.

Canonchet's death, as well as news of mounting losses, depressed Philip. Many Indians began to question the wisdom of Philip's war. Awashonks, the Sakonnet leader who had given information to the colonists about Philip's early war plans, again contacted her colonist friend Benjamin Church. Although the Sakonnet were part of the Wampanoag people, some of Awashonks' men led the settlers back to Philip's hiding place. Philip escaped, but this new episode of betrayal was the beginning of the end.

LEFT: The colonists conjured up images of King Philip as a demon figure who roamed the deep wilderness scheming to end what they perceived as their harmonious relations with the Indians. After their final battle against the Indians, the colonists financed another phase in their campaign to colonize New England and claimed new areas of land and enslaved resistant Indians, selling them in Spain and the Caribbean. The widow and son of King Philip were sold for thirty shillings apiece in the West Indies.

ABOVE RIGHT: The New England Confederation of Massachusetts, Plymouth, Rhode Island, and Connecticut glorified their war on the Wampanoag and their allies.

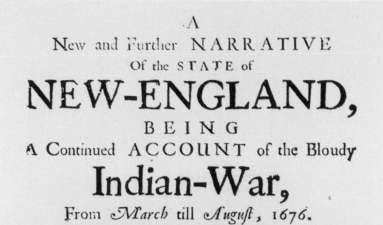

Day after day, Philip's forces disintegrated. The Narragansets were being wiped out and the Nipmucks were surrendering all over New England. In a dramatic episode, the Nipmuck chief, Shoshanim, and 180 of his people marched into Boston with their war chief Matoonas and his son bound with ropes. The colonists tied Matoonas to a tree, and Shoshanim shot and killed him. Shortly thereafter in southern Massachusetts, Wetamoo's body was found in the Taunton River; the colonists took her head to Plymouth and mounted it on a pole.

When one of his Indians suggested they surrender to the English, Philip had the man killed. This set in motion the final act of treason against him. The dead man's brother, Alderman, betrayed his chief to

the English and led Church and a band of soldiers to Philip's camp. The Wampanoag chief was shot by Alderman as he fled during the ambush.

The troops decapitated and quartered Philip's body and carried his head back to Plymouth, where it remained on public display for twenty-five years. His wife and son were sold into slavery in the West Indies. Church gave Philip's scarred hand to Alderman, and for months, Alderman exhibited it in a pail of rum "to such men as would bestow gratuities on him." King Philip is remembered as one of the first Indians who perceived the immense threat that white European settlers posed to the Indians, realizing that the only hope for his people was to drive white settlers from the continent.

ABOVE: Present-day Assawompsett Pond has changed over the centuries; it was formerly the Great Swamp where a dramatic battle was fought during King Philip's War.

RIGHT: Photographed in 1923 in the town of Ipswich, Mrs. Stafford was directly descended from Massasoit and King Philip. Other descendants of the Algonquian-speaking tribes of the region still survive, as do many of their words and phrases. The Algonquian word *podunk*, for example, meaning a corner of isolated land, was given to a Massachusetts town but also came to signify any remote locale.

CHAPTER THREE

Popé and the Pueblo Revolt

PRAYER TO THE CORN MOTHERS

Our old women gods, we ask you!
Our old women gods, we ask you!
Then give us long life together,
May we live until our frosted hair
Is white; may we live till then
This life that now we know!

—PRAYER TO THE FIRST MOTHERS OF THE TEWA PEOPLE,
FROM WHOM EACH CHILD RECEIVES THEIR SOUL AT BIRTH

IN 1680, A PUEBLO INDIAN MEDICINE MAN NAMED Popé led one of the most dramatic uprisings in Native American history, slaying hundreds of Spaniards and driving the rest back to Mexico in terror. In two weeks, the Pueblo people put an end to eighty-two years of Spanish rule that had enslaved the Pueblo Indians as laborers and Christians. Although the Pueblo Indians occupied about seventy different sites and many of the tribes were widely separated by the steep-walled mesas and plains and valleys that covered their homeland, which ranged from present-day Arizona to the mountains east of the Rio Grande, Popé successfully led an uprising of more than sixteen thousand of his people. He led Zunis and Hopis from the rocky deserts of the West, as well as the Keres, Tewas, and other tribes who lived along the Rio Grande. The white settlers called Popé's people the Pueblos because of the citylike appearance of their buildings.

Popé was born around 1630 in Grinding Stone in present-day New Mexico. He was born during squash-harvesting season, hence his name, which means literally "ripe squash." Little is known about him, except that by the time he appeared as a political force, he was an old Tewa medicine man living in the San Juan pueblo, the reconstruction of which can be found near present-day Española, New Mexico. All his life, Popé had resisted Christianity, which the Spanish friars had tried with significant success to force on the Indians. He had struggled to keep traditional Indian beliefs alive among his people.

The spiritual base on which the Pueblo Indians constructed their society was a conviction, permeating all phases of their life, that everything they could possibly comprehend—the natural forces around them, their own thoughts, distances across land, animals, birds, reptiles, and every action, thought, and being of which they were aware—was part of a great living force and contained a spirit that existed everywhere. Whatever existed on earth came from an underworld to which it eventually returned in death. Passage between the two regions was through the waters of a lake; the first men had emerged into the world, bringing spirit with them from below, at a place called Sipapu. Each community constructed a stone-lined pit within its *kiva,* or temple, which symbolically represented Sipapu but was thought to be the actual passage between the lower world and the earth above.

ABOVE: Prior to the Indian revolt, the Spanish authorities had been unfamiliar with Popé. He had been only one of numerous medicine men who, despite the friars' stern proscriptions of native beliefs, had continued to defy white men with secret religious practices that were held in a stone-lined pit within the community's *kiva*, or temple.

RIGHT: The stone-lined pit within a kiva was believed to be the actual passage between the lower world and the earth above. Pueblo Indian tribes today struggle to maintain their ancient beliefs, a task that becomes more difficult with each generation. At the Santo Domingo Pueblo in New Mexico, Native Americans perform their new year's dance much the same way as they have for seven hundred years.

Popé's job as medicine man was to be in charge of ceremonial activities and to keep watch against the evil spirits that brought sickness and death to the pueblo. Wearing the paw of a brown bear glove-fashion over his right hand, he used prayers, chants, and mystic paintings of colored corn meal that he sprinkled on the ground of the kiva to charm the spirits and heal his patients. If a patient died, it was proof of the strength of the spirit; if they lived, it was proof of the power of the doctor. As guardians of life and health, medicine men were often given political influence.

During the years before the war, serious droughts began to affect the Southwest and many Indians wondered if their gods were angry. With the coming of the drought, Popé's religious activities began to take on political overtones. He held secret meetings in the pueblo and said that the gods were speaking against the friars. He told his people that the Spaniards must leave Indian land.

As Popé's meetings became more frequent and increased in size, his influence spread. When word reached the mayor of Santa Fe, he had Popé arrested and flogged in the public plaza of the capital. Popé was released but rearrested shortly thereafter and publicly flogged again. It was too late. Popé's warnings were already being spread in pueblos throughout New Mexico. Alarmed, the Spanish governor sent troops to all the settlements to stop Indian religious rituals and arrest all the medicine men. Forty-seven leaders, including Popé, were arrested. They were charged with witchcraft and sorcery; three were hanged. Popé and the others were whipped and jailed. The governor's actions inflamed the

ABOVE: When they were old enough, unmarried Hopi girls tradition-ally wore their hair in a "squash blossom" style on both sides of their heads; married women wore their hair down. The Hopi are the most renowned of the surviving, un-Christianized Native American commu-nities. They live high up on flat-topped desert mesas. One of their villages, Oraibi, is reputed to be the oldest continually inhabited town in the United States—occupied for perhaps a thousand years.

LEFT: New Mexico's earth-colored Taos pueblo appears today just as it did hundreds of years ago during the golden age of the pueblos, which lasted through the thirteenth century. Some Pueblo tribes were divided into two groups, known as the Summer People and the Winter People, and each group took turns at running the town for half the year.

through the passageway that came from the lower world. In feathers and shining paint, the gods breathed fire and called for a Pueblo revolt. They ordered Popé to set the date of the uprising and to send each chief a cord of maguey fibers with a number of knots tied in it to signify the days left before the revolt.

Popé did as he was told, sending cords to the chiefs that set the date for the uprising on August 11, 1680; to the chiefs whose loyalty he questioned, he sent cords signifying a later date. The plan worked. Informers revealed the wrong date to the Spanish, who were unprepared when the Indians began attacking and killing Spanish poachers in the fields, burning buildings, and marching toward Santa Fe. When the Indians attacked en masse, the fighting was bitter and frantic. After several severe battles, the Indians abandoned their struggle and fled.

Despite their victory, the Spanish had no desire to remain in Santa Fe. They began an exodus to the south, hoping to find safety in the Spanish colonies on the Rio Grande. Their hopes were dashed. As they moved south, every pueblo they encountered stood empty of Indians—all of whom had joined the revolt. Soon there were dead Spaniards everywhere. Starving, those refugees who managed to escape finally made it to safety in El Paso.

The entire province of New Mexico once again belonged to the Pueblo people. Four hundred Spaniards had been killed, including twenty-one of the thirty-three Franciscan friars in the territory, along with almost four hundred Indians. Popé and his followers moved into the ruins of Santa Fe. After dividing the spoils of war, Popé ordered the people to forget what they had learned from the Spaniards and return to the ways of their ancestors. In each pueblo, the medicine men washed the Christianized natives clean of their baptisms with yucca suds.

Sadly, the Pueblo people's victory soon crumbled. Their attempts to return to a way of life that had existed before the coming of the Spanish was impossible. Popé was consumed by his success and became dictatorial, demanding obedience and insisting that others bow in his presence. He used prisoners as servants and even rode around in the Spanish governor's carriage. War broke out between the Pueblo tribes loyal to Popé and those who opposed him. Although he was deposed, Popé was eventually restored to power eight years before his death.

Twelve years after the revolt, in 1692, the Spaniards returned in sufficient force to reconquer the area. After four years of sporadic but heavy, brutal fighting, Spanish rule was restored, although it was never again as strong as it had been before the revolt.

Indians, who demanded that their leaders be released or they would rise up and kill every Spaniard in the province. The frightened governor complied.

Popé continued to hold secret meetings with other medicine men and chiefs. First, he told them, they must cleanse their ranks of informers. As an example, he dramatically announced at a meeting in San Juan that he suspected his own son-in-law, Nicolas Bua, the Spanish-supported Indian governor of the pueblo, of being a spy for the white men. The next day, the Indians stoned Bua to death in a cornfield.

During the summer of 1680, Popé told his followers that it was time for action. To battle the Spanish Christians, he planned to use the powers he possessed through his connection with the spirit world. Before an entranced audience, he summoned three native gods—Caudi, Tilini, and Tleume—whom the Indians believed had entered the kiva

LEFT: Pueblo Indians, especially the Hopi, had a very strong clan system that traced descent through the females. A man married a woman of another clan, to which his children would belong. The husband was a guest in his wife's mother's house, and while he was responsible for his children's education, they were not members of his clan.

ABOVE: The land of the New Mexico and Arizona Pueblo Indian tribes is rugged country, with scorching summers and fiercely cold winters. Despite the area's low rainfall—the greater part having less than twenty inches per year—Pueblo Indian tribes excelled at dry farming and developed varieties of corn that modern technology has never equaled. Where there was water available, they developed irrigation techniques.

CHAPTER FOUR

Pontiac's War in the Wilderness

MAN'S SONG

It is my form and person that makes me great.
Hear the voice of my song—it is my voice.
I shield myself with secret coverings.
All your thoughts are known to me—blush!
I could draw you hence, were you on a distant
island; though you were on the other hemisphere.
I speak to your naked heart.

—CHIPPEWA LOVE SONG

PONTIAC WAS BORN AROUND 1720, PROBA-bly in an Ottawa village on the north side of the Detroit River. It is believed that one of his parents was an Ottawa and the other a Chippewa or a Miami. Pontiac grew into a tall, powerfully built chief and coura-geous forest warrior who wore beads in his ears, a decorative stone in his nose, and silver bracelets on his wrists. Using clever strategies, he led eighteen powerful tribes from Lake Ontario to the Mississippi River in a devastating war against the English colonists, which saw the capture of eight out of twelve British forts in Indian country, the forced abandonment of a ninth, and the prolonged sieges of two others.

For almost a century, the Indians along the Atlantic seaboard had been facing the pressure of settlers who demanded Indian land. But beyond the Appala-chian Mountains, in the interior of the continent, settlers had not yet appeared in great numbers, and the sit-uation was different. Relations between white men and Indians had been deter-mined almost entirely by the commercial fur trade. The French traders were the first to arrive and were welcomed by the Indians because they wanted nothing but furs and land on which to build their posts. In return, the French provided the Indians with guns, ammunition, and European trade goods.

The fur trade created jealousies, however, and brief wars among the various tribes were common. These tribes included the Menominees, Winnebagos, Sauk, and Foxes in the lake regions of present-day Wisconsin and Illinois; the Miamis, Weas, Kaskaskias, Mascoutens, Piankashaws, and Kickapoos along the rivers in both Illinois and Indiana; the Shawnees and Delawares in Ohio and western Pennsylvania; and the Chippewas, Potawatomis, and Ottawas, who were previously members of one tribe but were now scattered, along with the Hurons, in villages from the southern shore of Lake Erie to the northern peninsula of Michigan.

About 1738, when British traders began to appear along Lake Erie and in other areas on the west side of the Allegheny Mountains, the French monopoly of the fur trade ended. The British offered the Indians better goods for less furs and drew some Indian villages away from the French. Other natives, however, including Pontiac's band of Ottawas, remained loyal to the French during the fifteen-year power struggle that ensued between them and the British. When the French abruptly ceded power to the English, the Indians were baffled. In 1760, the British sailed up Lake Erie and raised the flag over Fort Detroit.

The treatment of the Indians under Sir Jeffery Amherst, commander in chief of the British forces in North America from 1760 to 1763, was far from generous. The French had always provided for the Indians, but Amherst's shortsightedness prevented him from seeing the advantage of placating the Indians by distributing hunting ammunition,

LEFT: The Ottawa chief Pontiac believed that his people would be able to return to their traditional ways if the white men could be cleared out. He nearly succeeded in driving the British out of the Old Northwest region.

ABOVE RIGHT: In the late 1660s, the French established secure trading posts in the western Great Lakes region. There they exchanged European trade goods and weapons with the Woodland Indian tribes for beaver furs and other pelts. The traders grew in numbers, and soon, Jesuit missionaries arrived along with emissaries of the French king. Among the new arrivals were licensed traders who had been given diplomatic responsibilities.

provisions, and other small gifts of goodwill. The Indians became increasingly angry at the English, and Pontiac's passionate speeches gave voice to their resentment, increasing the number of his followers.

Sometime during the winter of 1762 to 1763, Pontiac heard Neolin, the Delaware prophet, speak. Neolin told listeners that he had taken a long journey and had met the Master of Life himself. The Master was unhappy because the natives had allowed themselves to fall victim to the white men. Twisting the story slightly, the prophet reported that the Master of Life bore no ill will toward the French but meant only the English when he referred to the whites.

With this new and important religious backing, Pontiac announced to his warriors that he was going to lead an attack against the British at Fort Detroit. The British, however, found out about Pontiac's scheme to gain friendly entrance into the fort and ambush the inhabitants once inside. Forestalling the frustration of his warriors after this first attempt was foiled, Pontiac announced that the war would commence immediately. If they could not get into the fort, they would kill all the Englishmen outside it, keep the post surrounded, and force the British to surrender. At the same time, he deployed the Hurons and Potawatomis and ordered them to intercept any Englishmen coming toward the fort. He also sent war belts to tribes throughout the Ohio Valley and the Great Lakes region to proclaim the start of the uprising.

ABOVE: Chippewa women utilized a basic loom to weave clothing, using a slow, laborious method called finger-weaving.

RIGHT: When the Woodland Indian tribes, including the Potawatomi, lived near the Carp River, which winds through upper Michigan, they were nomadic foragers. Women were primarily responsible for gathering vegetables; the men were responsible for hunting and fishing. Once settled in warmer climes to the south, around A.D. 1500, they cultivated and harvested corn, beans, and squash.

Allied with the French residents along the river who supplied ammunition and other goods, the Indians stunned the British and achieved shattering victories. The English garrison at Fort Sandusky on Lake Erie was captured by the Ottawas and Hurons; Potawatomis overwhelmed Fort St. Joseph in southwestern Michigan and killed or captured all its defenders; a war party from Detroit, joined by Miami Indians, forced the surrender of Fort Miami in present-day Fort Wayne; the Delawares and the Mingoes, acting on Pontiac's orders, massacred settlers and fired on forts in Pennsylvania's Monongahela Valley.

As other tribes joined the conflict and triumphs continued, the damage to the English grew to devastating proportions. In less than two months, the British lost every Ohio Valley and Great Lakes post except for two—Detroit and Fort Pitt—but both of those were under siege. The English supply route along Lake Erie to Detroit was no longer safe, and the line of communication from Pittsburgh to Niagara was gone. When France ceded to Britain at the end of the French and Indian War in 1763, Pontiac's hopes were dashed; he realized that French troops would never appear to help him. He held his people together, however, and the number of warriors increased as new bands joined.

Amherst offered a thousand pounds for the death of Pontiac, and a few weeks later, in a fit of anger, he doubled the price. All this proved unnecessary, because as time passed and the Indians seemed further and further from victory, Pontiac's prestige began to diminish. In addition, the French inhabitants of the region turned their backs on the Indians, causing doubts among the native chiefs who had been allied with Pontiac. One by one, bands sought entrance to Fort Detroit and surrendered and then made their way off through the forests to their homelands.

Desperate, Pontiac made several attempts to rally his support. In a badly planned attack, he sent warriors in canoes against a schooner that had arrived at the fort; many Indians were killed and wounded. The defeat further weakened Pontiac, and a few days later, a large band of Potawatomis defected and returned to their home. Dissension spread rapidly.

LEFT: The dividing point between the Mississippi and St. Lawrence watersheds is in Ohio. Until the 1660s, the Iroquois controlled the approaches to the French trading posts on the St. Lawrence River, which made traveling between the western lakes and the east hazardous for the Woodland tribes.

When Pontiac received word from the commander of the French Fort de Chartres on the Mississippi River that the French had come to an agreement with the English and implored the Indians to stop their war, he was demoralized. The next day, he sent a note to Major Henry Gladwin, the British commander at Fort Detroit, which read, "My brother, the word which my father has sent me to make peace I have accepted; all my young men have buried their hatchets. I think you will forget the bad things which have taken place for some time past. Likewise I shall forget what you may have done to me.... I, the Chippewas, the Hurons, we are ready to go speak with you when you ask us.... If you are as king as I, you will make a reply. I wish you a good day. Pontiac."

In the ensuing months, Pontiac attempted to revive the conflict, but he was thwarted. The British were pacifying tribes with promises of trade faster than Pontiac could stir them to fight. The British eventually put Pontiac at ease by convincing him that they now saw him as a brother, instead of an enemy, because Pontiac had signed in peace for all his people at Detroit. They still attempted, however, to undermine what little influence he had left by deliberately playing him up. Rumors spread among the Indians that Pontiac was now being paid ten shillings a day by the British. With that, his prestige was almost gone.

White injustices against the Indians were revived with the return of peace. But Pontiac was now taking the side of the whites and counseling peace. In time, members of his village began to turn against him. Rumors circulated that his former warriors were physically beating him. Finally, in May 1768, Pontiac wrote to the English at Detroit that his young men had "shamed" him and that he was being forced to leave.

With only his family and a small following, Pontiac traveled to Illinois country. On April 20, 1769, he visited a small trading post in Cahokia, a French village on the east side of the Mississippi River opposite St. Louis. Unarmed, he was accompanied only by a Peoria Indian. For some reason that has never been established, the Peoria suddenly stabbed Pontiac. The great war chief fell to the ground and died.

Pontiac is remembered for his eloquent powers of oration, which succeeded in uniting many different tribes, as well as his ability to think in terms of long-range strategy; as a war chief, he planned and acted decisively not simply for the moment but for the achievement of large and distant aims. Most of all he is remembered as a daring and shrewd leader who led a vast confederacy of powerful tribes that almost succeeded in driving the British out of the Ohio-Illinois region.

CHAPTER FIVE

Maquinna of Vancouver Island

SONG

Don't you ever
you up in the sky
Don't you ever get tired
of having the clouds
between you and us?

—NOOTKA

ON MARCH 28, 1778, A GROUP OF NOOTKA Indians stood on the shore of Friendly Cove, now known as Resolution Cove, on the west coast of Vancouver Island in what is now British Columbia, Canada. They waited and watched as two tall ships sailed toward them. Among the group was Maquinna, a Nootka chief who was about to become his tribe's primary contact with the European traders who would soon become plentiful in the region. Maquinna was the son of a Nootka chief and had succeeded his father in 1778. His birth date is unknown.

The Nootka were fishermen and the only whale hunters in British Columbia. Because of the mild climate on Vancouver Island, they wore very little clothing. Both men and women wore aprons and robes made from cedar bark or sea otter fur, as well as blankets woven from dog or mountain goat hair, which were dyed yellow, black, and turquoise blue. Most of the time, they went barefoot.

The Nootka also liked to adorn their bodies with jewelry. In their ears and noses they wore copper hoops, beads, abalone shells, and whale teeth; bangles and bracelets decorated their necks and arms. For great events, such as feasts and war parties, they painted their faces white, black, and red. Their hair generally flowed down to their shoulders, but sometimes they brushed it back, holding it in place with bracelets and furs.

On that day in March 1778, the villagers debated among themselves about the approaching ships. Some thought the ships were floating islands. Others believed that they carried one of the Nootka gods, who was now returning to live among them. Maquinna already knew differently; some of his people had been in contact with Spanish explorers, and Maquinna himself owned two silver spoons that he had probably received from Spanish sailors.

Maquinna, his face painted and wearing a feather headdress, paddled out to the first ship accompanied by another chief and six men from his tribe. The British trading vessel was the *Discovery*, manned by Captain James Cook. Behind it was the *Resolution*, commanded by Captain George Bly. The young George Vancouver was also on the voyage.

In return for Maquinna's gifts of furs, Captain Cook presented the chief with several brightly colored blankets. Maquinna was so pleased with the exchange that he took off his sea otter coat and presented it to Cook, who in turn handed Maquinna his captain's hat. That night, the ships' crews came ashore, and the villagers welcomed them with a wolf dance. The newcomers stayed in the area for about a month while their ship was overhauled.

In return for salmon and furs, Maquinna received axes, knives, and other types of metal objects, all of which increased his wealth and prestige among his people. When the British left the island, they had more than three hundred furs, many of them sea otter, a very valuable fur in China, which was where they were headed.

LEFT: In a portrait entitled "Macuina 'Xefe de Nutke'" from Viage el Estrecho de Fuca, 1802, Maquinna is wearing a woven hat that portrays harpooners pursuing a whale.

ABOVE RIGHT: The Nootka produced fine basketry and art work. To weave, they twined left strands through warp strands that were hanging free from a "half loom"—a loom with an upper bar but no lower bar. They also used this technique to produce blankets and other garments with elaborate designs, woven with yarn made from cedar bark or mountain goat wool. The Salish Indians sheared a breed of small woolly dog to obtain wool to combine with the bark.

After Cook's departure, other traders who had heard about the valuable furs poured into the villages, and Maquinna controlled trade with the newcomers. In time, he opened up passes to the inland sea on the west side of Vancouver Island. Soon his power and influence spread far into the interior and along the western seaboard.

In 1786, Captain Strange, who worked for the East India Company, decided to leave an agent in Maquinna's village while he and his crew returned to sea. The man he chose was John Mackay, the surgeon's helper, whom the chief trusted because Mackay had cured Maquinna's son of a skin infection. Mackay was to stay in the village a year to study the native language and treat minor illnesses. He tried to teach the Nootka about the Christian religion but had little success; Maquinna was quite happy with the Nootka gods.

As the year wore on, the friendship between Mackay and Maquinna began to wear thin. When Mackay became too friendly with the native girls, Maquinna expelled him from the village and made him live in a hut. The following year, when the sailing ship arrived to pick him up, Mackay was unwashed, unshaven, and dressed in tatters.

During the next ten years before his death in 1795, Maquinna dealt extensively with British, American, and Spanish traders. During that time, the Spanish managed to confiscate a British ship and take prisoners and to build a Spanish settlement in the Nootka village of Yuquot. Maquinna accepted this as best he could and sold a piece of land in Yuquot to the Spanish captain, Martinez.

ABOVE: Within clans, there were lines of descent that could be traced back to an animal with spiritual significance. This ancestral lineage gave individuals rights to certain insignias or crests as well as to dances, songs, rituals, hunting rights, and so on.

RIGHT: The Northwest Coast Indians took the same artistic care with their dress as they did with their art; the Nootka basketry hat is a sign of personal adornment.

After a ceremony held by Martinez and four priests to dedicate the land to the Spanish crown, Maquinna's brother, Chief Callicum, paddled his canoe out to the Spanish ship to reprimand the Spaniards for taking British prisoners. Fearing attack, Martinez ordered Callicum to come on board. When Callicum refused, Martinez fired at the chief and killed him.

That night Maquinna sent four men, their bodies blackened with charcoal, out to the Spanish boats to cut the anchors. As the vessels drifted out to sea, the Spaniards tried to attack, but were unable to see the painted bodies of Maquinna's men in the darkness. Later, Maquinna ordered every house in Yuquot burned to the ground and led his people to Opistat, the village of Callicum's father-in-law.

Eventually, the Spaniards regained Maquinna's favor by bestowing gifts on him and singing a song of his praises: "Great is Maquinna. Maquinna is a great chief. Spain loves Maquinna." With the chief's permission, the Spanish built a new settlement, but eventually, the British flag was raised in Friendly Cove.

For quite some time, no new settlers arrived in the area and all that remained in Friendly Cove was a few ruins. By 1795, Maquinna had brought his people back to live in Yuquot and rebuilt his village. Later that year he fell ill and died. Maquinna is remembered as a powerful and influential leader who helped open up the abundant Northwest Coast region to Europeans.

NATIVES OF THE NORTHWEST COAST

❧

The Indians who inhabited the coast of present-day British Columbia and southern Alaska built great wooden houses and massively carved totem poles and created abundant culture. Their economy was founded on fishing and hunting, using both the land and the sea resourcefully. Though their culture was almost destroyed by contact with Europeans and the fur trade, the coastal Indians have seen a renaissance, with new totem poles being raised and ceremonies being revived.

The Indians of the Northwest Coast were few in numbers. When Spanish and English mariners arrived in the region in the late eighteenth century, they estimated the population at less than one hundred thousand. The nations of the Northwest Coast included the Tlingit in the north along the southernmost islands and coastal reaches of Alaska; the Haida, Tsimshian, Kwakiutl, Bella Coola, Nootka, and Coast Salish of the coastal regions and islands of British Columbia; the Salish and Chinook of Puget Sound and the lower Columbia River; and the Yurok, Karok, and Hupa of northern California. These people were scattered in independent villages and maintained only temporary alliances. The villages themselves were divided by the rivalries of kinship groups.

In wealthy villages, slaves, taken from rival tribes, made up approximately one-third of the population. Social classes above the slaves were divided into commoners and nobles. Occasionally, as among the powerful chiefs of the Haida of the Queen Charlotte Islands, there was a sort of royalty.

Related families lived together in plank houses, with house posts and door poles carved and painted with the family crest. The coastal dwellers even put carvings and designs on the walls and supporting posts of their houses.

Carvings on totem poles symbolized the ancestral titles of the village chiefs. By claiming rights to the animal crests carved on the poles, the chiefs were actually saying that they were great providers of food and comfort. The height of a pole, together with its bold designs, indicated that there was a mighty chief in the village who could cause great things to be done.

Their art included carved wooden masks, woven baskets, and engraved and painted copper plating that colorfully depicted their lives. These lives continued relatively undisturbed until the fur trade brought civilization and, ultimately, ruin to the coastal people.

LEFT: Tlingit children in Alaska as well as children in other tribes in the Pacific Northwest observed their parents, learning fishing and other skills necessary to survive in the challenging climate of Pacific coastal areas.

ABOVE: The settlement of the New World was a slow process, with people crossing from Siberia into Alaska over a period of fifteen thousand years or more. Totem poles were erected by the descendants of these early natives of the Northwest Coast to establish status or in memory of their departed chiefs. Crests and insignia are carved on these red-cedar poles.

TRIBES OF CANADA'S GREAT WHITE NORTH

❧

The Eskimos, including the Aleuts of the Aleutian Islands, are the most widely known of North America's native peoples. Eskimos, however, are a distinct and separate people from the Indians who inhabited some regions of the far north. These inland Indian tribes of the great black forests that bordered the treeless tundra included the Naskapi in Labrador, the Algonquian-speaking Cree, and the Athapascan-speaking Chipewyan around the south and west shores of Hudson Bay, as well as various groups, such as the Blackfoot, who lived in the broad interior of northwest Canada ranging from the Hudson Bay to the Pacific.

The Athapascans were essentially a woodland people, dependent on hunting and fishing for their existence. The northern tribes occasionally hunted caribou on the tundra, but the Arctic seacoast held little interest for them, and access to the southern plains was blocked by the powerful Cree tribes.

These northern peoples are still the least known of the Indians of North America and include such tribes as Yellowknives, Dog-ribs, Slaves, Beavers, Hares, and Carriers. Their names are generally descriptive titles applied by white men: The Beaver and Hare were named for their principal game and the Yellowknives for their copper instruments, while the Carriers got their name from a tribal custom requiring a widow to carry the ashes of her dead husband in a basket for three years.

Currently there are approximately five hundred thousand officially recognized Indians in Canada, many of whom live on reservations. Representatives of these tribes belong to the Assembly of First Nations, an activist group that is working toward further recognition of Indian rights by the Canadian

government. While Canada does not share the exceptionally violent history of the United States in its relations with native peoples, for two centuries Canada's Indians have become increasingly dependent on white government.

Ovide Mercredi, Cree chief and the leader of the Assembly of First Nations, has discussed a "national act of disobedience," in which natives would challenge white authority by ignoring federal and provincial laws that restrict native hunting. "My challenge...is to turn grievances into solutions," he says. "The onus is as much on us as it is on the federal and provincial governments."

OPPOSITE, TOP: Cree tribes, as well as other natives of the Great Lakes region and south central Canada, used the birch tree in constructing their homes. Cree hunters were known for their tactic of rolling sheets of birch bark to fashion megaphones that they used to amplify moose calls.

OPPOSITE, BOTTOM: During the seventeenth century, the Cree Indians were the principal tribe encountered by British fur traders who pushed down from the Hudson Bay and by the French, who followed the St. Lawrence and Great Lakes canoe route from Montreal.

ABOVE LEFT: Blackfoot tepees contained two flaps, called "ears," on either side of the smoke hole. Created by the Plains Indians, this allowed for adjustments to the wind and permitted the hole to be closed completely if desired. The tepees were decorated with symbols of their owners' powers.

LEFT: The Blackfoot Indians were a large and powerful people, comprised of three closely related tribes. The British traders gained the allegiance of the Blackfeet by the late eighteenth century, but the settlers who came to obtain their own furs in the nineteenth century met only with resistance from the Blackfeet.

POTLATCH

All coastal Indians participated in a ritual known as potlatch, though the Kwakiutl and northern peoples were known to be the most extravagant. The object of potlatch was to give away or destroy more wealth than one's rival, however some tribes also used the ritual to honor in-laws. If the potlatch giver was a powerful chief, he might attempt to shame his rivals and gain everlasting admiration from his followers by destroying food, clothing, and money. Sometimes he would even seek prestige by burning down his house.

A chief was never content with the amount of respect he was getting from his followers and from neighboring chiefs. Therefore he felt an obligation to justify and validate his chiefly pretensions. The best way to do this was to hold a potlatch. Each potlatch was given by a host chief and his followers to a guest chief and his followers.

The host chief arranged the material to be given away in neat piles. This included fresh and dried fish, fish oil, berries, animal skins, blankets, and other valuables. The

chief then boasted to the guests about how much he was going to give away. The host chief might say, "I am the only great tree. Bring your counter of property that he may try in vain to count the property that is to be given away." Then the chief's followers would warn the guests: "Do not make any noise, tribes. Be quiet or we shall cause a landslide of wealth from our chief, the overhanging mountain."

The guests would belittle what they received and vow to hold a return potlatch at which their own chief would prove he was greater. An ambitious chief and his followers had potlatch rivals in several different villages at once. Considering all villages as a single unit, potlatch stimulated a ceaseless flow of prestige and valuables moving in opposite directions.

ABOVE: Carved and painted Kwakiutl house fronts often depicted tribal myths. The designs were formalized for artistic balance.

LEFT: In 1900, a photographer recorded this Haida potlatch ceremony.

At some potlatches, blankets and other valuables were not given away, but were destroyed. Sometimes successful potlatch chiefs held "grease feasts" at which boxes of candlefish oil were poured on the fire at the center of the house. As the flames roared up, dark grease smoke filled the room. Sometimes the house caught fire and burned to the ground, a great show of wealth. The guests sat quietly or even complained while the wealth destroyer chanted, "I am the only one on earth—the only one in the whole world who makes this smoke rise from the beginning of the year to the end for the invited tribes."

CHAPTER SIX

Tecumseh, the Greatest Hope

But hear me: A single twig breaks, but the bundle of sticks is strong.
Someday I will embrace our brother tribes and draw them into a bundle
and together we will win our country back from the whites.

—TECUMSEH SPEAKING OF THE GREENVILLE TREATY OF 1795

NO NATIVE AMERICAN BEFORE HIM HAD ATTEMPT- ed to unite tribes on the scale visualized by Tecumseh, the visionary Shawnee chief. Despite tribal rivalries, he conceived of all Indians from Canada to the deep South as one people, not as divided nations. He denied the right of whites to purchase land from whichever tribe would sell it, insisting upon common ownership by all Indians. He pursued his vision of a single confederacy, embodying the eastern Indians' last hope of saving their culture.

Tecumseh was born in 1768 in the Shawnee village of Piqua on Mad River, about six miles southwest of present-day Springfield, Ohio. His mother, Methoataske (meaning "turtle laying eggs in the sand"), was part Creek and part Shawnee. His father was a Shawnee warrior named Puckeshinwa, meaning "I alight from flying" or "one who drops down." Tecumseh, meaning "flying" or "springing across," signified, like his father's name, membership in the Great Lynx Clan, a patrilineal Shawnee clan. Members of the Great Lynx Clan were responsible for guarding the rear of a returning war party. Tecumseh's name was translated as "crouching lynx," "panther," or "shooting star."

During his boyhood, early on in his training as a warrior, Tecumseh distinguished himself. When his courage was tested in real warfare, however, he was found severely wanting. At the age of fifteen, he joined his brother Cheesekau in a skirmish on the banks of the Mad River. When the blood started to flow, Tecumseh ran. His shame about the incident reinforced his resolve never to run from an enemy again.

In 1783, the numerous tribes of Ohio held a great council and vowed to defend their country against all invaders. While still a teenager, Tecumseh participated in attacks on white settlers who were moving onto Indian lands in the Ohio Valley and Great Lakes region now known as the "Old Northwest." The Indians took up arms to protect their territories on the Ohio River, attacking supply boats and wagon trains moving west from Fort Pitt.

During one such attack, all the settlers were killed except one, who was taken prisoner and tortured to death with burning brands. Tecumseh, who watched silently, was horrified. When he expressed his horror to the other warriors, he did it with such passion and eloquence that they vowed never again to burn captives.

After falling from a horse during a buffalo hunt, Tecumseh was unable to keep pace with war parties and despaired of becoming a successful warrior—to the point of attempting suicide. But it was also during this dark period that Tecumseh made the first of many journeys that would lay the groundwork for the unification of Indian peoples. Still recovering from his injury, he joined Cheesekau in riding to his mother's Shawnee village in Missouri. He also visited the Shawnee of southern Illinois and the Miami tribe in Indiana.

When Cheesekau was killed by white men on the Tennessee frontier in 1789, Tecumseh joined the Miami chief Michikinikwa and a force of Miami, Shawnee, Potawatomi, and Chippewa Indians in fighting against the militiamen in the area. During the next several years, Tecumseh was a prominent figure in some of the worst slaughters during the Indian Wars.

Tecumseh's outrage was effectively fueled during the next several years. In 1795, following a successful surprise attack by the U.S. Army against the Indians at Fallen Timbers, on the Maumee River, general in chief "Mad Anthony" Wayne established Fort Wayne, Indiana, and forced the chiefs of twelve different tribes to sign the Greenville Treaty. The agreement ceded most of Ohio, a portion of Indiana, and distant enclaves including Detroit to the United States in exchange for annuities amounting

LEFT: Tecumseh was reputed to have been a great athlete and hunter as well as a great war chief.

RIGHT: In addition to iron-pipe tomahawks, guns were also carried as weapons during Tecumseh's war. These required a horn and pouch for carrying and loading gunpowder.

to $10,000. Tecumseh was furious with the council of chiefs who had signed and refused to accept the treaty. Instead, he split with Blue Jacket, the Shawnee chief, and became the leading hostile chief in the region.

Finding support among the Delaware, Tecumseh lived in Indiana until about 1805. In 1796, he married a woman named Manete who bore him a son before she left due to their quarreling. The boy was called Puchethei, meaning "crouching or watching his prey." During the final years of the eighteenth century, Tecumseh became close to a woman named Rebecca Galloway, who taught him world history. Tecumseh eventually proposed marriage to her and she consented, but only under the condition that he abandon Indian ways and live like a white man. The great chief told her that he could never abandon his people.

By 1809, Tecumseh was actively seeking to unite the divided tribes into one mighty alliance and made the first of his epic journeys to speak to tribes throughout the Old Northwest and the South. Many of the old chiefs resisted, preferring to preserve the Greenville Treaty, but most of the young warriors were excited by his plans. To the west, he gained support from the Sauk and Winnebago tribes; to the south, from the Creeks, Cherokees, and Seminoles. By 1810, a thousand warriors were gathered at Prophet's Town, the village Tecumseh had established with his brother, Tenskwatawa the Prophet, who was the leader of a reform movement among the Shawnees. The reformers preached against adopting the white man's ways, and in particular, they promoted abstinence from alcohol. Oddly enough, however, the movement was against the proscribed use of medicine bundles, songs, and dances that were prominent features of Shawnee culture. Because of this, the Prophet's religion initially met with strong opposition but eventually became popular with the Shawnee and neighboring tribes.

When Tecumseh returned to Prophet's Town with his thousand warriors, he discovered that General William Henry Harrison, in his bid to secure Indiana's statehood, had persuaded a number of Indian chiefs to sell more land. Tenskwatawa had failed to oppose the treaty and his brother was outraged. When Harrison heard of the displeasure at Prophet's Town, he invited Tenskwatawa, whom he still believed to be the leader of the Indians there, to meet with him at Vincennes. Instead, Tecumseh arrived with four hundred warriors, much to the distress of the American troops.

On August 12, 1810, Tecumseh met with Harrison. As the general approached Tecumseh, he said, "Your father requests you to take a chair."

Tecumseh walked away and sat on the ground, declaring, "My father? The sun is my father, and the earth is my mother, and on her bosom I will repose."

He then addressed the council in his native language, which was translated by an interpreter: "...The white people have no right to take the land from the Indians, because they had it first; it is theirs. They may sell, but all must join. Any sale not made by all is not valid.... It requires all to make a bargain for all."

Harrison's attempts to placate Tecumseh only angered the chief, who called Harrison a liar. Harrison drew his sword and Tecumseh's warriors gathered around. Tecumseh led his warriors away and bloodshed was avoided.

The following day, Harrison again agreed to see Tecumseh. During this meeting, the two men sat next to each other on a bench; Tecumseh constantly moved down it, forcing Harrison to do the same. When the governor asked Tecumseh whether he would prevent a survey of the land, Tecumseh stated that he would "adhere to the old boundary."

ABOVE LEFT: When Tecumseh allied his Indian confederacy on the side of the British during the War of 1812, Tecumseh was given a commission as a brigadier general and was presented with a wool-bunting British flag.

RIGHT: During Tecumseh's final battle, soldiers spotted the Indians in a swamp. As the U.S. Army pressed forward through the under-brush, the battle mounted. Many could hear Tecumseh's voice over the fighting. "He yelled like a tiger, and urged his braves to the attack," a soldier said later.

Chiefs from the Wyandot, Kickapoo, Potawatomi, Ottawa, and Winnebago tribes voiced their support, while Tecumseh forced Harrison farther along the bench. Finally, Harrison protested that he was about to be shoved off. Laughing, Tecumseh explained that this was what the settlers were doing to the Indians. Tecumseh left Vincennes without reaching an agreement with Harrison.

During the next year, Tecumseh traveled more and brought new tribes into his alliance. He returned to Prophet's Town in 1812 to find that it had been nearly destroyed by Harrison's forces. He was furious with Tenskwatawa for leading the premature attack on Harrison's camp that had precipitated the town's destruction. After shaking him by the hair and threatening to kill him, Tecumseh cast his brother into exile.

The Indian confederacy finally came together in their final show of strength when they allied themselves with the British, against the settlers, during the War of 1812. The British gave Tecumseh an independent command of the Indian forces, and he was given a regular commission as a brigadier general. Tecumseh was a brilliant strategist, managing to trick many troops into surrendering.

Ironically, the inefficiency of the British commander cost Tecumseh many of his followers. And as the months went by and the British were forced to retreat farther and farther north toward Canada, it became clear to Tecumseh that his days were numbered. Prior to the final battle, he spoke to his remaining loyal chiefs: "Brother warriors, we are now about to enter into an engagement from which I shall never come out—my body

TENSKWATAWA, THE PROPHET

Tenskwatawa inspired fanaticism among his people and became the leader of the movement of which Tecumseh gradually gained control.

Contact with white civilization had a detrimental effect on the Shawnee, including the addiction of many Indians to whiskey. Although Tecumseh preached abstinence, one of the worst drunkards was his brother Laulewasika, whose name meant "rattle" because he was said to have a belt that he could transform into a rattlesnake. He also had a gruesome appearance, due to the loss of one eye.

In 1805, Laulewasika fell into a trance. When he awoke, he claimed to have spoken with the Master of Life. He changed his name to Tenskwatawa, meaning "the open door," and at a tribal council, he pronounced himself "the Prophet." He preached against the adoption of the white man's way of life, his tools and weapons, and condemned the use of alcohol. He promised the return of divine favor if the Indians returned to their traditional ways. Strangely enough, he also preached against the use of traditional Indian medicines and ceremonies, which caused opposition in the beginning, although his teachings eventually became popular among the Shawnee and many neighboring tribes. Like Neolin, the Delaware prophet of Pontiac's time,

LEFT: As twilight came to the countryside during the final battle, the dream of an Indian nation disappeared completely. Darkness halted the fighting and the Indians slipped away through the swamp. By then, Tecumseh was dead.

ABOVE RIGHT: Tecumseh's war was based on a popular movement led by his brother, Tenskwatawa. Tenskwatawa is said to have been an alcoholic who reformed after he had a vision. Soon afterward, he became a prophet.

shall remain on the field of battle." Unfortunately, his premonition was correct. He was struck in the chest by a bullet and killed during the Battle of the Thames.

Without Tecumseh to unite them, the Indians and their confederacy of tribes came apart. Though they remained loyal to the British, they were impossible to control. Tecumseh's Shawnees were forced westward by expansion, eventually settling in three distinct groups in Oklahoma. For years, the settlers were plagued by rumors that Tecumseh was still alive, reflecting the fearful respect in which he was held. The site of Tecumseh's burial continues to be a mystery, and he is still revered and highly regarded by the Shawnees today.

CHAPTER SEVEN

Osceola, Alabama-born Seminole Chief

LULLABY

Baby, sleep, sleep, sleep
Father has gone to find turtle shells
He said he will come back tomorrow
Baby, sleep, sleep, sleep

—CREEK

O SCEOLA WAS BORN BILLY POWELL IN 1804, in a village near the Tallapoosa River in Alabama. His mother was the daughter of a Creek woman and a white trader; his father is believed to have been a half-breed Scottish-Creek trader named William Powell. Although his people were Tallassees, who are members of the Creek Nation, Osceola was to become known as a brave Seminole warrior chief.

As the Seminoles fought in the malarial jungles and swamps of Florida against large American armies during the Second Seminole War, the country at length came to recognize Osceola as a patriot leader of a grievously wronged people. Before the end of the conflict, during which the U.S. government sought to remove the Indians from the Florida peninsula, Osceola had become a noble hero in the United States, celebrated even by his former enemies and memorialized in the names of new American towns and in the works of popular poets and authors.

Osceola's earliest years were spent among Indians whose resentments against the white settlers were rising rapidly. On the brink of the War of 1812, the Shawnee chief Tecumseh visited the Creeks and tried to convince them to join in the war against the foreigners. The Creeks split into prosettler (White Stick) and antisettler (Red Stick) factions, which led to the Creek War of 1813 to 1814.

Osceola was too young to join the warriors, but he watched as the Red Sticks of his village left for battle. A coalition of white soldiers, prosettler Creeks, and other Indian allies defeated the Red Sticks, and Osceola and his mother went into exile with other Tallassees and Creeks, who were driven from their homes by the settlers. They moved eastward toward the head of the Florida peninsula and settled among the bitterly antisettler Seminoles (Seminoles were largely Creeks who had moved to Florida to escape the settlers). By the time Osceola was fourteen, he and his mother had been captured during another Indian-American conflict; when they were freed, they resettled with their group near Tampa Bay.

During his youth, Osceola distinguished himself as a hunter and warrior and rose to the leadership of a small band of Tallassees who acknowledged him as their military leader, or *tustenuggee*. He received the Indian name Osceola, which means "black drink singer." The name referred to the cry that accompanied the drinking of an emetic known as "black drink." Among the Muskhogean-speaking peoples of the South, the black drink was both an important power, or "medicine," for spiritual purification and part of the annual thanksgiving ceremony. The black liquid, made by boiling the leaves of the cassina shrub, acted as a strong purgative and also caused exhilaration when taken in large quantities. Village leaders often took the black drink before councils to prepare their minds for debate, while warriors used the liquid to cleanse and strengthen their bodies for battle. The drinkers would take long draughts and then force themselves to throw up the liquid, sending up streams six to eight feet (2 to 2.6m) in the air. Osceola was probably an important participant in such ceremonies.

In 1819, the United States obtained Florida from Spain. By 1830, the Americans were seeking to remove the hostile Seminoles to Indian

LEFT: Osceola, the chief who led his tribe against strong U.S. government forces during the Second Seminole War, married an African-American woman of slave descent.

ABOVE RIGHT: This buckskin coat is believed to have belonged to Osceola.

Territory in the present state of Oklahoma. Some of the villages felt they had suffered enough trials in Florida and were not opposed to moving. Most of the other Seminole towns, including Osceola's village, tried to arouse the Seminole nation to oppose the removal.

According to the terms of several agreements signed between the Seminoles and the United States government, Osceola's group was to have been removed by 1833. In the confusion and expectation of having to leave their villages, few people planted gardens that year. The government failed to ratify the agreements until 1834; as food supplies dwindled and the Indians began pillaging white settlements, hostilities between the settlers and the Indians increased.

In addition, the Seminoles were retaliating against slave hunters who were seeking to remove blacks from their tribes. Scattered among them was a large black population, including both slaves and freemen. Many had been purchased by Indians from whites and had lived with

ABOVE: The death of Osceola did not end the Seminole War. Chief
Wild Cat joined forces with Alligator and others and fought on in
the hummocks and swamps. A succession of U.S. military leaders,
including Zachary Taylor, gradually drove the Indians farther into
the recesses of the Everglades.

RIGHT: Although most Seminole Indians were captured and shipped
to Indian Territory in the present-day state of Oklahoma, a handful of
survivors persisted. In August 1842, when the U.S. government finally
abandoned the struggle to root them out, more than three hundred
Indians were left in the wilds of the southern portion of the Florida
peninsula.

the Indians as dependents rather than slaves. The Indians had often intermarried with blacks and their children were considered free. Many blacks rose to high positions among their bands or established their own villages and became part of the Seminole nation.

The passage of the Removal Bill in 1830 began the process of forced emigration of Indians from east of the state of Mississippi to Oklahoma. The Cherokee, Creek, Chickasaw, Chocktaw, and Seminole tribes were coaxed, coerced, and forced into cooperating. Attempts to move the Seminoles resulted in a war that lasted twelve years. The Seminoles looked to Osceola for leadership. Osceola's boldness and uncompromising opposition to removal was winning followers among his people, and he became the spokesman for all Seminole chiefs, who were impressed by his ability to evade U.S. troops. They knew of his tactics of moving his people skillfully around the troops' flanks or into thick stands of undergrowth and trees where troops could not get them.

A dramatic story, the truth of which has never been established, describes an incident in which the U.S. government was trying to get the chiefs to sign an agreement to emigrate. Osceola walked angrily to the treaty table, drew his hunting knife, and drove it through the paper, pinning it to the table. He is said to have looked at the mutilated treaty and said, "That's your heart, and my work."

The most publicized feature of the Seminole Wars was Osceola's capture. The much-wanted leader had set up a flag of truce and, while he was meeting with the U.S. commander, was surrounded by troops. The manner of Osceola's seizure while under a white flag stirred a storm of protest throughout the country.

Still in his early thirties, Osceola died in a military prison three months after his capture. Knowing the end was near, he clothed himself

LEFT: George Catlin's painting of Osceola, whose war against the Americans lasted eight years and cost the U.S. government between forty and sixty million dollars, dates to the year 1838.

TOP RIGHT: In 1927 a photographer captured Seminole Indians in the Florida Everglades reenacting life on a nineteenth-century trading post. Some Seminoles who still reside in rural Florida say that they are often mistaken for Filipinos or some other nationality.

BOTTOM RIGHT: This photograph of Seminole dwellings was taken in 1928, but it represents how they had lived for several hundred years.

in full military dress: shirt, leggings, moccasins, war belt, bullet pouch, powder horn. He painted half of his face, neck, and throat, as well as his wrists, the backs of his hands, and the handle of his knife, red with vermilion—a custom practiced when an irrevocable oath of war and destruction was taken. He shook hands with his two wives, two children, the officers, and chiefs around him. Laying down, he held his scalping knife in one hand and placed his other hand across his breast. Then he quietly died.

The war went on. Wild Cat, Alligator, and other chiefs fought in the hummocks and swamps. But they were gradually driven into the recesses of the Everglades. When peace was made, most moved west to Indian Territory in Oklahoma. Several Seminoles remained in the region, resisting all inducements to emigrate.

CHAPTER EIGHT

Rival Chiefs Black Hawk and Keokuk

PRAYER TO THE GHOST

Here it is, the tobacco...
...This also I ask of you: do not cause us to follow you soon;
do not cause your brothers any fear.
I have now lit the pipe for you.

—WINNEBAGO

IN 1816, THE SAUK CHIEF BLACK HAWK WAS among those who signed a treaty confirming an earlier cession to the U.S. government of most of northwestern Illinois, southern Wisconsin, and part of eastern Missouri. "I touched the quill to the treaty," Black Hawk explained in his autobiography, "not knowing, however, that, by that act, I consented to give away my village." While Black Hawk had resisted signing for as long as he could, another Sauk chief, Keokuk, had urged compliance with the treaty; as a result, the tribe was divided. In 1832, Black Hawk went on the warpath in an attempt to save his village, Saukenuk. Black Hawk's War lasted only fifteen days and is considered the last of the Indian Wars of the Old Northwest.

About thirteen years Keokuk's senior, Black Hawk was born in 1767 in Saukenuk, at the junction of the Rock and Mississippi rivers, where Rock Island, Illinois, stands today. Saukenuk was located at the center of Sauk and Fox lands. The two tribes were treated as a single tribe, although they had migrated from different locations. Their long, bark-covered lodges and gardens of corn, beans, squash, and pumpkins dotted the banks of the Mississippi River from the mouth of the Wisconsin River in the north to Des Moines in the south. The river strip was a principal waterway for the fur trade. Although the Sauks and Foxes had long been familiar with French and Spanish traders, they were among the last to feel the pinch of the westward frontier movement.

During his youth, Black Hawk took his name after learning in a vision that his guardian spirit was a sparrow hawk. He was descended from civil chiefs but grew into manhood as a warrior. At fifteen, he won distinction by wounding his first enemy, a member of the Osage tribe, and was allowed to paint himself and wear a feather. Shortly thereafter, he joined his father in battle. "Standing by my father's side," Black Hawk recalled, "I saw him kill his antagonist, and tear the scalp from his head. Fired with valor and ambition, I rushed furiously upon another, smote him to the earth with my tomahawk— run my lance through his body—took off his scalp, and returned in triumph to my father. He said nothing, but looked pleased. This was the first man I killed!" By the time he was in his thirties, Black Hawk was leading armies of Sauks and Foxes in campaigns far from home.

Black Hawk's rivalry with Keokuk, which would eventually divide the Sauk and Fox tribes, began during the War of 1812. While Black Hawk was away fighting with Tecumseh and the British forces, the Sauks and Foxes were back at home falling under the influence of the white settlers. Seeking American protection from the fighting, some members of the tribe moved from the east side to the west side of the Mississippi River and established new villages on the Missouri River. Conveniently for the Americans, this removed the Indians from British influence, as well as from Indian land. Black Hawk returned home from battle in 1813 to find that the men who remained in Saukenuk had elected a new war chief; his name was Keokuk.

LEFT: In 1833, one of the most celebrated visitors to the eastern United States was the sixty-six-year-old Sauk chief, Black Hawk. Sauk, a shortened form of Osakiwug, means "people of the yellow earth," and it is believed that the Sauks once lived in Canada. Although the Sauks and the Foxes, or Meshkwakihug, meaning "red earth people," were originally separate tribes from different locations, they were treated as a single nation.

ABOVE RIGHT: George Catlin painted a portrait of White Cloud, an advisor to Black Hawk, in 1832.

Keokuk, whose name means "one who moves about alert," was a previously unnoticed member of the tribe. He was born in Saukenuk in about 1780 to a mother who is believed to have been half French. Already in his thirties, Keokuk did not possess military skills, and Black Hawk was surprised by news of his appointment to war chief. He was told that it had occurred at a council meeting held to discuss news that a hostile army of Americans was approaching the village. At the council, a majority decided to abandon Saukenuk and move to the west side of the Mississippi River, where others had already gone. Keokuk objected, volunteering to lead warriors in defense of the town should it be attacked, and made a rousing speech in favor of remaining in Saukenuk. The council consented that Keokuk should become a war chief.

An uneasy peace was established during the years following the truce signing in 1816, during which Black Hawk was misled by the government and unknowingly signed away Saukenuk. The frontier was rapidly moving westward, and the Sauks and Foxes were determined to retain their homes, which made them a potential menace. White settlers moved onto Indian hunting lands, chasing away game. To avoid starvation, the Sauks and Foxes invaded the hunting lands of the Sioux. The tribes quarreled, isolated settlers became involved, and enraged natives took white men's scalps.

Keokuk served as a delegate to the settlers, attempting to pacify them with promises of his tribe's cooperation. The settlers in turn showered him with gifts, which did not escape the notice of other members of the tribe. Some of the influential leaders saw the promise of presents and favors for themselves, and they felt that further opposition to the powerful Americans was short-sighted. Gradually, with American patronage, Keokuk's influence increased until he spoke in councils with the authority of a civil chief. At the same time, the Americans increased their pressure on the Indians to move west of the Mississippi before there was trouble.

Black Hawk met with Keokuk during this time to see what could be done, proposing that they offer the settlers another part of their land in return for the right to keep their village sites. Keokuk agreed, he claimed, and promised to go to Washington, D.C., or to put the matter to the "Great Father." Keokuk's visit to Washington, however, did nothing to solve the problems of the villages on the Rock River. In fact, Keokuk even signed away contested land west of the Mississippi River in Missouri. The

failure of Keokuk's trip filled Black Hawk with much bitterness. Black Hawk's enmity did not disturb Keokuk, who was determined to become head chief.

As the Sauks and Foxes took sides behind one of the two leaders, divided into camps, and debated whether or not to move, white settlers continued to take up land closer to the Rock River. The proximity of the settlers brought friction. Black Hawk complained that the white men entered Saukenuk with whiskey, got the Indians drunk, and cheated them out of horses and guns. Indians were randomly beaten by settlers.

The conflict stirred resentments of Indians throughout the region, but Keokuk urged them to have patience with the settlers. In 1827, Winnebagos, who lived north of the Sauks and Foxes, began to raid nearby settlements. When the U.S. government sent troops to the area, the Winnebagos called on the Foxes for help. Instead of aiding the Winnebagos, the Foxes under Keokuk's direction acted as spies for the U.S. Army. After the Winnebagos' defeat, Keokuk was rewarded.

The Winnebago uprising created a new crisis for Black Hawk and his followers, known as the British Band, who continued to refuse to migrate. "We were a divided people," Black Hawk recalled, "forming two parties. Keokuk being at the head of one, willing to barter our rights merely for the good opinion of the whites; and cowardly enough to desert our village to them. I was at the head of the other party, and was determined to hold on to my village, although I have been *ordered* to leave it...."

In 1831, U.S. militia was finally called in to force Black Hawk and his people from Saukenuk. The soldiers arrived to find the town deserted, and in their frustration, they leveled it by fire. Black Hawk and his people had evacuated during the night and crossed to the west side of the Mississippi River. The old leader was summoned to a meeting where he agreed to never return to Saukenuk and to submit to Keokuk's authority. Despite this agreement, Black Hawk, now almost sixty-five, decided to recruit new followers and return to Saukenuk with the group, which included women and children, the following spring to plant. Keokuk learned of his plans but could not stop them.

The U.S. government sent warnings to Black Hawk, who found refuge with the Winnebagos, demanding that he return to Rock Island. The messages, Black Hawk said, "roused the spirit of my band, and all were determined to remain with me and contest the ground with the war chief, should he come and attempt to drive us."

After finding out that he would receive no help from the British or from other Indian tribes, Black Hawk realized his mission was futile and

LEFT: Sauk and Fox wooden medicine dolls became part of the collection of the Chichester Museum in England in 1845.

ABOVE: According to some accounts, Keokuk, Black Hawk's rival for chieftainship of the Sauks and Foxes, announced in a council meeting that the U.S. government had made him supreme chief of the Sauks. Black Hawk reportedly struck him across the face. In 1834, George Catlin painted Keokuk on horseback in elaborate dress.

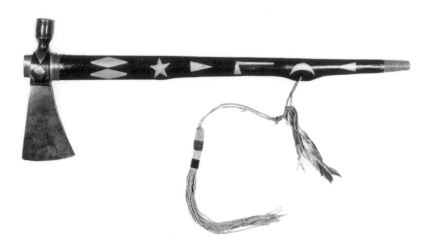

LEFT: A lead-pipe tomahawk that reportedly belonged to Keokuk was found in Oklahoma.

RIGHT: In 1900, this photograph, which includes Black Hawk's great-granddaughter (seated and wearing a kerchief on her head), was taken in Iowa.

BELOW: The Winnebagos of Wisconsin were allies of both Tecumseh and Black Hawk, legendary chiefs who led their people in resistance to U.S. settlers.

decided to turn back. But it was too late; there would be no turning back. The U.S. Army was already coming after him. After weeks of pursuit and violence culminating in a bloody battle on the banks of the Mississippi, where hundreds of Indians were killed, Black Hawk surrendered.

With Black Hawk and other principal leaders behind bars, Keokuk met with the U.S. government to negotiate a lasting treaty. To increase his influence among the natives, Keokuk was named civil chief by the commissioners, who then obtained from him a cession of six million acres (2.4 million ha) of Sauk land running along the Mississippi River in the present state of Iowa.

Eventually, Black Hawk and the other prisoners were released from prison. They toured some of the cities in the East and then returned home. During the following years, as Black Hawk watched Keokuk sell more Sauk and Fox lands in Iowa and grow wealthy and powerful, his final complaint was that Keokuk, the man who opposed and helped to defeat him, was now the white-appointed head of their tribe.

Black Hawk died in 1838 at the age of seventy-one. Keokuk died in 1848 in Kansas, where he had moved after selling the Sauk and Fox lands in Iowa. A bronze bust of Keokuk was placed in the capitol building in Washington, D.C.

Lakota Chief Sitting Bull

Many buffalo, I hear, many buffalo, I hear,
They are coming now, they are coming now,
Sharpen your arrows, sharpen your knives!

—LAKOTA

SITTING BULL WAS BORN A HUNKPAPA Lakota in 1830 in what is now the state of South Dakota. Elected leader of all the Lakota, Sitting Bull fought long and hard to keep his people off reservations. He also became known as the warrior who killed General George Armstrong Custer at Little Bighorn.

Sitting Bull was born Hunkesni, a Lakota word meaning "slow." The Hunkpapa Lakota were Tetons, the name given to the western division within the Great Sioux nation. Hunkpapa means "those who camp by the entrance." The Hunkpapa and other Lakota tribes lived by following and hunting buffalo across the Great Plains, which provided them with all their food and clothing. War between the different tribes on the plains was also a way of life. Among the Cheyenne, Crow, Shoshone, Snake, and Arapaho, stealing and raiding was considered the best way to get new horses.

Hunkesni was fourteen years old when he first participated in the practice known as "counting coup." A warrior counted coup when he rode up right next to his enemy in battle and struck him with a coup stick, which was a long, thin, decorated wooden stick. The

Lakota believed that this was a more important way for a warrior to prove that he was courageous than killing his enemy, because it showed his willingness to brave death. After the first time Hunkesni counted coup, his father passed his own name of Sitting Bull on to his son. His father took the name Jumping Bull.

ABOVE: Sitting Bull, along with his wife, family, and followers, fled into Canada a few months after the Custer massacre. U.S. government envoys urged him to attend a council in Boston that was designed to lure him back into the United States. Sitting Bull refused the invitation.

LEFT: U.S. military leaders and war correspondents singled out Lakota Chief Sitting Bull as the native genius behind General Custer's massacre.

Like his father, Sitting Bull was said to have been able to communicate with animals. One time, he awoke from a nap in the woods to the sound of a woodpecker. He knew the Great Spirit was sending him a message to lie still. A great grizzly bear emerged from the woods and stood over Sitting Bull, but left without hurting him. As a gesture of gratitude, Sitting Bull claimed the Bird People as his relatives and began to write songs. He developed a beautiful singing voice and performed at tribal ceremonies.

The Lakota believed that a sacred force pervaded every aspect of their lives, so that their very existence was sacred. One of the sacred rites of the Lakota was called *hanblechyapi*, meaning "crying for a vision," or "vision quest," through which a young man sought guidance from the sacred powers. After purifying himself and under the guidance of a holy man, the vision seeker fasted until he received some portent of his sacred power, or "medicine."

When he was fifteen, Sitting Bull went on his vision quest. Naked and alone, he sat on a hill for three days. On the third day, he heard a voice telling him that he was in the presence of the Great Spirit. The medicine man of the tribe, Moon Dreamer, was impressed with this vision and decided that Sitting Bull was ready to take the final step into manhood and could participate in the rite of passage known as the Sun Dance, which took place every summer. During the Sun Dance, a skewer was passed through the skin of Sitting Bull's back and fastened to a pole in the ground. Other young men of the tribe were fastened in the same way, and they danced and sang, proud to show how much pain they could endure. They believed that this pleased the Great Spirit and proved how brave they could be. They bore the scars from the Sun Dance with pride, having earned their place among other men of their tribe.

Sitting Bull joined the Cheyenne in their war on the invading white settlers, and from then on his reputation as a warrior grew. Following the Sand Creek Massacre, a brutal massacre of a Cheyenne encampment by the U.S. Cavalry in 1864, he was named military chief of the Lakota. At the Sun Dance ceremony in 1865, the Cheyenne and Arapaho joined the Lakota at Sitting Bull's initiation. Chiefs Running Antelope, Loud-Voiced Hawk, Four Winds, and Red Horn all took part in smoking a ceremonial pipe with Sitting Bull. First, they pointed the pipe toward the earth so it would continue to hold them together. Then they pointed it toward each of the four winds to make sure that no ill wind would blow against them. Last, they pointed it toward the sun so it would light their way. At the same ceremony, they appointed Crazy Horse second in command after Sitting Bull.

The next several years on the Great Plains were bloody and violent. Indians from many different tribes battled with white settlers and soldiers. A treaty in 1868 established a Lakota reservation bounded by the North Platte River and the Bighorn Mountains. This land consisted of parts of the states now known as North and South Dakota, Nebraska, Wyoming, and Montana. The Black Hills, which the Lakota considered sacred, were part of this land. Sitting Bull wanted no part of this reservation for his people, because he did not trust the white settlers or the U.S. government. When he heard that Red Cloud, a powerful Oglala chief, was taking part in a council to decide where the Lakota reservation should be, Sitting Bull said, "The white people have put bad medicine over Red Cloud's eyes."

Sitting Bull and his people remained on their land, but despite the Treaty of 1868, the Americans soon decided they wanted to run the Northern Pacific Railway right through the Indian territory. The United States government maintained that they had a right to do this because of the boundaries that were specified in the treaty. But for twenty years following the signing of the Treaty of 1868, the specifics would be argued between the Indians and the government. The government maintained that the Indians had misunderstood the treaty while the Indians believed that they had been deceived by the government or perhaps deliberately

ABOVE: Lakota Sun Dancers painted their bodies in preparation for the ceremony.

LEFT: From 1835 to 1837, George Catlin executed a painting entitled *Self-Torture in a Sioux Religious Ceremony.* **To some, the spiritual rites of many Native American tribes might seem tortuous. During the Lakota Sun Dance, some men ran skewers through the muscles in their chests and backs, swinging from thongs until the skewers were torn loose.**

RIGHT: In 1871, a Cheyenne named Red Cloud (not the famous Oglala chief by the same name) painted a buffalo hide to depict a battle between his tribe and a party of Shoshoni.

LEFT: Montana's Glacier National Park preserves the dramatic, mystical landscape that was home to the Plains Indians.

ABOVE: Thousands of pioneers traveled along the base of Scott's Bluff by way of the Oregon and Mormon trails. The deep ruts left by their Conestoga wagons can still be seen today.

River, ready to fight the U.S. Army. Sitting Bull was an important chief in the camp, but there was no single leader. At the Sun Dance ceremony at the Rosebud encampment, Sitting Bull offered one hundred pieces of skin cut from his body in exchange for the Great Spirit's help in their fight. When the cutting was finished, Sitting Bull began a three-day-long dance under the sun. On the third day, he fell to the ground in a trance and had his most famous vision: As he stared up at the sky, he saw hundreds of soldiers. Their bodies were falling down toward the earth. A voice said, "I give you these because they have no ears." Sitting Bull interpreted this as meaning that these were the white men who would not listen to the Indians. He also took it as a sign that there would be a great battle, which the Indians would win.

A few days later, after the Indians had moved their camp to the Little Bighorn River, they were attacked by the U.S. Cavalry. Thousands of Indians poured into the valley, the dust from the horses' hooves making it almost impossible to see. When the fighting was over, not one of the 260 cavalrymen was left alive, including General George Armstrong Custer.

Because the government was not able to capture Sitting Bull or the other chiefs who fought beside him, action was taken against the Lakota on the reservations: they were declared prisoners of war. Sitting Bull met with a colonel from the cavalry, but this attempt at a peace talk ended in a fierce battle that lasted for two days. Sitting Bull knew he would never be left to live in peace and eventually moved to Canada, where he and his followers set up camp in the Pinto Horse Hills, which would later become the province of Saskatchewan. He remained there until the Canadian government, worried about having so many new Indians within its borders, told him to return to the United States. The fifty-year-old Sitting Bull surrendered at Fort Buford, in what is now North Dakota, and was arrested for killing Custer.

In the meantime, Sitting Bull's name had become well known around the world. Following his release from prison after almost two years, he attended the celebration of the opening of the Northern Pacific Railway. There he made a speech in the Lakota language saying that he

misled by interpreters. As the railroad progressed, the Indians stepped up their attacks.

As soon as gold was discovered in the Black Hills, miners rushed in. The government knew it would be impossible to keep the miners out, so they decided to force the Lakota to sign a new agreement. At the same time, herds of buffalo started to disappear as more settlers moved onto the Plains. Sitting Bull, however, still rejected the idea of giving up the land that the Indians had lived on for generations. The government declared all Indians who refused to move "hostile."

Attacks on Cheyenne and Oglala (one of the seven subtribes of Lakota) villages by the U.S. Army gave Indians west of the Missouri River cause to unite. In 1876, fifteen thousand Indians gathered on the Rosebud

ABOVE LEFT: In 1886, Buffalo Bill Cody and Sitting Bull posed for a photograph together. Sitting Bull was a star attraction of Buffalo Bill's Wild West Show. The chief was particularly impressed with the talents of sharpshooter Annie Oakley, who was another star attraction; it was only the promise that he would get to see her every day that persuaded him to join the show for a season.

hated all white people. The interpreter quickly made up another speech on the spot, and Sitting Bull received a standing ovation.

In 1883, he joined a Wild West exhibition and went on a nationwide tour of eighteen cities in which he was exhibited as Custer's killer. Then he joined Buffalo Bill Cody's Wild West Show, where he was paid fifty dollars a week for his part in the show. Cody went to great lengths to treat Sitting Bull with dignity. He never required the chief to participate in the show's mock battles, which were staged with large casts of Indians and cavalrymen. During each performance, Sitting Bull was announced with great fanfare and would ride alone into the arena, where for a few moments he was spotlighted as the sole attraction. Afterward, Sitting Bull always gave the money he had earned to children who were waiting for him outside the stage door. Rather than join Buffalo Bill for a European tour, however, Sitting Bull returned to his reservation. When he arrived, Sitting Bull was outraged to discover that the reservation had been divided up into six smaller nations consisting of much less land.

When Sitting Bull's name appeared on a list of names of people belonging to a new religion called the Ghost Dance, a warrant was issued for his arrest because somehow this innocuous group seemed to threaten the U.S. government's authority. Sitting Bull was killed by two Indian offi-

How Sitting Bull Got His Name

O ne day, Sitting Bull's father, who was later known by the English name Returns Again, and other hunters were out on the plains, preparing to cook the meat of a buffalo they had just killed, when they heard a voice nearby. The men grabbed their weapons, instantly ready to fight the enemy. Stunned, the hunters glimpsed their visitor—a lone buffalo, lumbering toward the campfire, speaking human words.

Returns Again knew much about spiritual matters and could communicate with animals. He realized that they were in the presence of the Great Spirit, who sometimes appeared in the form of a buffalo bull. Returns Again was the only one who could understand what the buffalo was saying: "Tatanka Yotanka, Tatanka Psica, Tatanka Winyuha Najin, Tatanka Wanjila,'' the Sioux words for "sitting bull, jumping bull, bull standing with cow, lone bull." To the Sioux, these terms stood for the four stages of life: infancy, youth, adulthood, and old age.

Returns Again knew the names spoken by the Great Spirit would have spiritual powers, so he decided to give up his own name and call himself Sitting Bull. When he honored his son by passing the name on to him, Returns Again took the name Jumping Bull.

ABOVE: "What have we done that the white people want us to stop?" asked Sitting Bull, in his frustration. "We have been running up and down this country, but they follow us from one place to another."

cers of the reservation during the struggle to remove him from his home. After his death, fighting between Sitting Bull's followers and the authorities ensued for several hours. Eight Hunkpapas, including Sitting Bull's son Crowfoot, and six police officers were killed.

Without Sitting Bull, the Hunkpapas left their camp and joined the Minneconjou camp of a chief named Big Foot. The cavalry tracked them down, however, and forced the whole group to Wounded Knee, South Dakota. On December 29, 1891, cavalry troops surrounded them, and the entire camp of three hundred Indians was wiped out during the massacre at Wounded Knee.

ABOVE: A year after this photograph was taken of Lakota leader Big Foot's men in the summer of 1890, they were killed, along with three hundred other Indian men, women, and children at Wounded Knee in South Dakota.

RIGHT: The last known photograph of Sitting Bull was taken in 1890.

CHAPTER TEN

Crazy Horse, "A Good Day to Die"

PRAYER

Father, Great Spirit, behold this boy! Your ways he shall see!

—SIOUX

CRAZY HORSE WAS BORN IN 1841 DURING the season his people recorded as the winter of the Big Horse Steal (the seasons and years were named after the most memorable events of each specific time period). He was named Curly and his birthplace was on Rapid Creek, east of the Black Hills in South Dakota. As a child, Curly was set apart from the other Lakota Sioux because of his pale complexion and light wavy hair. As an adult, he was set apart as a fearless warrior and revered mystic, the chief who fought with Sitting Bull at Custer's Last Stand. He was a formidable adversary of the cavalry and the white settlers who moved across the Great Plains during the middle to late nineteenth century.

Curly's people, like Sitting Bull's, were the Lakota, or Teton, Sioux, the westernmost arm of the Dakota nation. The Lakota were divided into seven subtribes, including the Hunkpatila, of which Curly was a member. Each tribe was autonomous except in matters affecting the Lakota nation as a whole. The Lakota adopted a seasonal migration pattern that mirrored the habits of the buffalo, which were plentiful on the Plains until their whole-

people fled north to escape the sickness. When he was ten, Curly sat with the women and children behind the warriors at a council meeting between U.S. agents and chiefs from the Lakota and Cheyenne tribes. At this council, the Indians signed a treaty agreeing to stop molesting settlers as they moved west on the Oregon Trail and to allow forts to be built on their land. Conquering Bear, the chief of Curly's tribe, signed for all the Lakota, although the Sioux could not understand how one chief alone could sign for all their people. The Indians now called the Oregon Trail the "Holy Road" because it could not be touched.

As a young man, Curly witnessed a great deal of violence against his people, which fueled his resentment toward whites. It also strengthened his resolve as a warrior, and when he was still in his teens, Curly sought guidance from sacred powers in the ritual called "crying for a vision" or "vision quest."

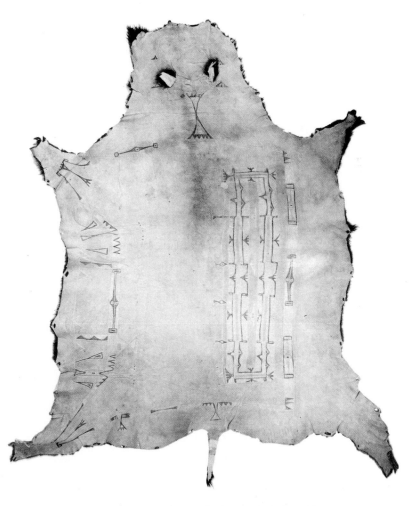

sale extermination was perpetrated by the white man during the late nineteenth century. War was also a constant feature of Sioux life, as they defended their hunting lands against the Crow, Pawnee, and Shoshoni.

Because of his unusual looks as a child, Curly was watched closely by his father, a holy man of the Hunkpatila band named Crazy Horse. When Curly was born, his umbilical cord was cut away and placed in a protective amulet fashioned after a turtle, to symbolize longevity. His ears were pierced during the first Sun Dance ceremony held after he could walk. At five, Curly received his own clothes and his umbilical amulet and was known as a "carry your navel" child. The protection of the cord was thought to grant protection to the child.

When Curly was still young, a cholera and smallpox epidemic hit the Plains, brought by the forty-niners bound for California seeking gold. His

ABOVE: The eagle feathers in Crazy Horse's headdress were believed to be imbued with the bird's spiritual powers.

LEFT: According to Marie Sandoz in her book, *Crazy Horse*, a legitimate photograph of the Hunkpatila chief has never been found.

RIGHT: A painted buffalo robe was purchased by an American collector from Crazy Horse's wife at the Rosebud reservation in 1890.

ABOVE: The agate fossil beds in the present state of Nebraska (which is from an Indian word meaning "land of flat water") are surrounded by lush grasslands.

LEFT: Pursuing well-mounted Lakota warriors across the rocky landscape of the Dakotas, General Alfred Sully christened this country the "badlands," claiming that it looked and behaved like "hell with the fires out."

Black Elk, an Oglala holy man and Curly's cousin, described the powers: "...Perhaps you did not know that he received most of his great power through 'lamenting' which he did many times a year, and even in winter when it is very cold and very difficult. He received visions of the Rock, the Shadow, the Badger, a prancing horse, the Day, and also of Wanbli Galeshka, the Spotted Eagle, and from each of these he received much power and holiness." At a victory dance following a battle, Curly's father gave him a new name, singing, "I give him a great name, I call him Crazy Horse."

Crazy Horse's bravery in battle brought him much honor, and he grew to be a respected warrior. Wearing his thunder medicine paint, he joined the Cheyenne and led warriors in frequent clashes with soldiers who guarded emigrants flooding the Holy Road. During a ceremony at a great council lodge painted with sacred designs, the greatest of the elders—or Big Bellies—named American Horse, Young Man Afraid of His Horses, Sword, and Crazy Horse the new chiefs, or "shirt-wearers," of the tribe. An old man then instructed the shirt-wearers on their duties: to promote harmony, to be generous, and to always place the people before themselves. Ironically, Crazy Horse would have to return his shirt after a serious incident during which he participated in violence in an argument over a woman.

Americans continued to move onto Indian land and peace dwindled. In 1864, the flames of violence were lit when the U.S. Army led a

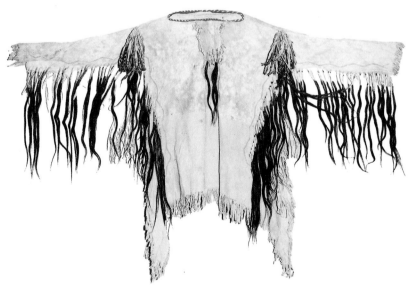

Instead of seeking the guidance of a holy man, Curly went out alone. For three days he lay on gravel, stripped to his breechcloth, with sharp stones between his toes to keep him awake. Curly had a vision in which a light-haired warrior on horseback instructed him not to wear a war bonnet or tie up his horse's tail before battle; he should also cast dust over his horse before fighting and should never take anything for himself from the battle.

OPPOSITE, LEFT: Oglala chief American Horse was an important ally of Crazy Horse's and Sitting Bull's and was initiated as chief on the same day as Crazy Horse. According to some reports, he was present when Crazy Horse died.

OPPOSITE, RIGHT: Crazy Horse's war shirt, a symbol of bravery and rank, was made of antelope skin and decorated with pendants of human hair. The fringes may represent the coups he struck, the scalps taken by him in battle, or the people in his tribe that depended on him.

ABOVE: Frequent clashes between the Cheyenne—allies of the Lakota in their common struggle against the U.S. government's usurpation of Indian land—and the U.S. army culminated in November 1864 when the cavalry made a barbaric surprise attack against a group of friendly Cheyenne who were camped under a truce flag at Sand Creek under the leadership of Chief Black Kettle. More than 130 Cheyenne, mostly women and children, were killed.

THE CHEYENNE LEADER BAT

No leader of the Cheyenne during the mid-nineteenth century was more famous to both settlers and Cheyenne than Bat, a hook-nosed, six-foot-three (2m) war leader. Bat was famous because he was invulnerable in battle due to a magic headdress made for him by Ice, a medicine man. While he wore it, bullets and arrows could not touch him. He proved this time after time by riding back and forth in front of the enemy while they fired at him and missed. This greatly inspired his fellow warriors. The only thing that could remove the magic from

Bat's headdress was if he were to eat something removed from a cooking pot with an iron instrument. If he broke this taboo, it would take long rites of purification to restore the bonnet's medicine.

One night before a battle, Bat was a guest in a Lakota lodge, and the cook, who was unaware of the taboo, removed food from the skillet with an iron fork. Bat did not notice this until he had already eaten. The next day, he did not go into battle. When the chiefs came and told him he was needed to inspire the warriors, Bat explained about the broken taboo. He said, "I know that I shall be killed today." Then he painted himself with war paint and put on his headdress, mounted his horse, and rode toward the enemy. He was shot from his horse. Then he was carried back to the tents, where he died at sunset.

---

barbaric attack on a group of friendly Cheyennes at Sand Creek who were under the leadership of their chief, Black Kettle. Approximately 130 Indians, mostly women and children, were killed.

These flames were fanned during Red Cloud's War, which successfully prevented settlers' passage from Fort Laramie along the Powder River to the gold fields of Montana. Red Cloud, a chief of the Oglala tribe, refused to be pushed aside and held forts along the trail under virtual siege for two years. Young chief Crazy Horse distinguished himself during this war when he led groups of five hundred warriors in attacks on the forts. In 1868, the government surrendered, the forts were dismantled, the troops moved out, and the Powder River country, including the Black Hills, was established as unceded Indian territory. But for twenty years following, the specifics of the Treaty of 1868 were argued between the Indians and the U.S. government. Disagreements about land boundaries caused major controversies, with the Indians believing they had been deliberately deceived by the government as to the contents of the treaty. The U.S. government insisted that the Indians had simply misunderstood what they had signed.

The wars reached a climax during the 1870s after gold was discovered in the Black Hills. The Sioux had to be persuaded to sell out, their sacred Black Hills having been guaranteed to them by treaty. The

Pawnees, Crows, and Shoshonis allied with the U.S. government against their old enemies of the Plains. The Lakota and their Cheyenne allies were under the leadership of Crazy Horse and Sitting Bull.

In June 1876, the main body of unpersuaded Sioux moved west and established a new camp on the Little Bighorn River following a battle at Rosebud Creek in southern Montana. Two days later, their camp was attacked by a regiment of cavalry, led by General George Armstrong Custer. Short Bull, who was present that day of the battle, saw Crazy Horse as the fighting started: "I looked to where he pointed and saw Custer and his blue coats pouring over the hill. I thought there were a million of them.

" 'That is where the fight is going to be,' said Crazy Horse. 'We'll not miss that one.' He was not a bit excited; he made a joke of it. He wheeled and rode down the river, and a little while later, I saw him on his

---

RIGHT: Little Big Man served as Crazy Horse's lieutenant and at one time threatened to kill the first chief that spoke for selling the Black Hills. After surrendering with Crazy Horse, however, his allegiance shifted. Some accounts assert that Little Big Man helped to set a trap for Crazy Horse by holding his former friend's arm as a cavalryman thrust a bayonet into him, killing the chief.

pinto pony leading men across the ford. He was the first man to cross the river. I saw he had the business well in hand. They rode up the draw and then there was too much dust—I could not see anymore."

The cavalry was defeated, and Crazy Horse was shouting, "Today is a good day to fight, today is a good day to die." Custer died in the battle along with more than 260 of his men. Not one soldier was left alive. Following the battle, Crazy Horse rode off alone to a butte near Reno Creek and engraved a horse and snake with lightning marks in the sand, the signs of his visions.

Inevitably, the huge Indian camp divided. Many Indians returned to their reservations and were forced to sign away the Black Hills on the threat of having their rations stopped. Crazy Horse held out, his people freezing and starving in the snow. Red Cloud's nephew Sword led an Oglala delegation from the reservation to beg Crazy Horse to surrender. Shortly thereafter, Spotted Tail, Crazy Horse's uncle and a prominent Oglala chief, led 250 Brule Lakota to Crazy Horse's camp to ask for surrender. Crazy Horse, seeing his people truly divided, stayed away from camp during Spotted Tail's visit. He left a message saying he would bring his people in when weather permitted.

When the weather cleared, Crazy Horse led nine hundred of his followers through the valley singing the peace song of the Lakota. Following his surrender, however, old rivalries resurfaced, and he attracted a surprising number of enemies. They advised the authorities to arrest Crazy Horse, who was exasperated by affairs at the Red Cloud reservation and was threatening to take his people north again.

When it became clear to Crazy Horse that he was being led to jail, he drew a knife, slashing Little Big Man, who had been one of his lieutenants, across the arm. American Horse and Red Cloud screamed,

LEFT: Made a chief of the Oglala on the same day as Crazy Horse and American Horse, Sword was the nephew of Chief Red Cloud, whose two-year war against the government succeeded in establishing the Black Hills as unceded Indian territory—at least for a while.

ABOVE RIGHT: From 1866 to 1868, Oglala chief Red Cloud and his followers, along with Cheyenne allies, successfully laid siege to army-built forts along the Bozeman Trail, which led through Indian land in Wyoming to newly established centers in Montana. Red Cloud's War eventually forced the army's surrender and evacuation of the forts, which were dismantled.

"Shoot to kill!" Crazy Horse was stabbed by a cavalryman and died. The Lakota gradually came to realize that they had killed their great warrior and chief out of fear and jealousy. One elder said later, "I'm not telling anyone—white or Indian—what I know about the killing of Crazy Horse. That affair was a disgrace and a dirty shame. We killed our own man."

When the Lakota were moved to a new reservation in Missouri, Crazy Horse's father stole his bones and wrapped them in a buffalo robe. He placed them in an unknown place near Chankpe Opi Wakpala, Wounded Knee Creek. Red Feather, Crazy Horse's brother-in-law, said, "His father hid his bones so that not even my sister knew where it was buried. Before he was buried a war-eagle came to walk on the coffin every night. It did nothing, only just walked about."

CHAPTER ELEVEN

Chief Joseph and the Nez Perce Retreat

LEADER OF THE NEZ PERCE DURING THE struggle to defend their homeland, Chief Joseph was a peaceful man whose story has inspired generations. Greatly outnumbered and pursued by the U.S. Cavalry, Joseph led his people in a gallant but vain attempt to reach Canada, where they had hoped to find sanctuary. The absence of any aggressive acts on the part of Joseph's people sets the Nez Perce conflict apart from all other Indian wars.

Joseph was born in 1840 in a cave near where Joseph Creek forks from the Grande Ronde River on the border between Washington and Oregon. His Indian name was Heinmot Tooyalakekt, meaning "thunder rolling in from the mountains," although he was baptized Ephraim by a Christian missionary living with the Indians. As the settlers' influence among the Nez Perce increased during the nineteenth century, a division was created between the settled, Christian Nez Perce and the "heathen," nontreaty faction.

The Nez Perce were a peaceful people who fished in the Columbia River and sometimes hunted buffalo. Christian missionaries taught them to farm. They were most renowned as great travelers, especially following the acqui-

ABOVE: The Nez Perce (French for "pierced noses") called themselves simply "The People," or Nimipu, as did most other North American Indian tribes. In 1805, William Clark and Meriwether Lewis were the first white men to encounter the tribe.

LEFT: "The earth was created by the assistance of the sun, and should be left as it was....The country was made without lines of demarcation and it is no man's business to divide it...." —Chief Joseph

sition of horses in the early eighteenth century. Through selective breeding, they developed the famous spotted Appaloosa pony and traveled south to the Plains and to the Northwest to visit coastal tribes.

Joseph's father, also called Joseph, was one of the antitreaty chiefs that met with the settlers in 1863 after gold was discovered on Indian land. Young Joseph was fifteen when he accompanied his father to this meeting. The Christian chiefs signed a treaty in which the Nez Perce sold 90 percent of their land to the U.S. government, but old Joseph refused to sign, calling it the Thief Treaty. He then went home and hammered stakes

CHARLO, FLATHEAD CHIEF

After his father, Victor, died in 1870, Charlo became head chief of the Flatheads, a tribe that lived in the Bitterroot Valley of western Montana. His Indian name was Small Grizzly Bear Claw, and in his younger days, Charlo was a fearless warrior and hunter.

When he still lived in the Bitterroot Valley, Charlo not only welcomed white settlers to live with his people but also risked his life to protect them. When Chief Joseph led his people on their retreat toward Canada, he sent word to Charlo that he needed help and supplies. Joseph thought their common struggle might unite their two peoples.

Instead of helping Joseph, Charlo sent word back to his old friend to stay clear of Flathead country and not to hurt any settlers in it. Otherwise, he said, Flathead warriors would be sent out to defend the white settlers against the Nez Perce. The U.S. government later forged Charlo's signature on a treaty and took away his land.

Under Charlo's leadership, the Flatheads resisted moving out of the Bitterroot Valley until 1891. The tribe then moved north and set up camps around the Jocko River, where they have continued to live ever since. The Charlo family reign ended with the death of Charlo's great-grandson, Paul Charlo, in 1957.

---

around their land in the Wallowa Valley to create a boundary. They lived there in relative peace as the settlers moved closer.

In 1871, old Joseph died. He told young Joseph, "Never forget my dying words. This country holds your father's body. Never sell the bones of your father and your mother." Joseph said that he would protect his father's grave with his life.

In 1876, the U.S. government told Chief Joseph that he and his people must leave the Wallowa Valley and go to the Lapwai Indian reservation in Idaho. Some of the young Nez Perce leaders wanted to fight the white men. A council was held, attended by Joseph and Ollokot from the Wallowa, Red Owl and Looking Glass from the Middle Fork of the Clearwater, White Bird from the Salmon River, and a powerful warrior, holy man, and orator named Toohoolhoolzote from the Snake River region. After speeches by Looking Glass, Red Owl, and the renowned warriors Rainbow, Five Wounds, and Grizzly Bear Ferocious, the Nez Perce voted against war.

It was only after much conflict with the U.S. government and disagreement within their own tribe, however, that the Nez Perce agreed to go to the reservation. They knew that they would be no match for the forces of the U.S. Cavalry. But the younger members of the tribe were furious, and while Joseph was away on a hunting trip, they singled out four settlers against whom the Nez Perce had particular grievances and killed them. Soldiers retaliated and the violence escalated out of control.

Joseph decided that the only alternative to a war in which the Indians would surely be defeated was to lead the Nez Perce to Canada. The soldiers could not follow them across the border into another country, and the Indians would then be free. But the United States would not let them go.

General O. O. Howard, a one-armed hero of the Civil War, was sent to capture Chief Joseph and force the Indians onto the reservation. From June until October 1877, Chief Joseph was pursued by the U.S. Army as he and his tribe fled toward Canada. His forces numbered only two hundred warriors, and they had few rifles, most of them taken from dead soldiers, and bows and arrows. The U.S. Army had modern weapons, including cannons. Chief Joseph had the additional problem of caring for almost six hundred women and children.

The chase covered more than a thousand miles of rugged mountain territory as Chief Joseph and his people moved through Montana, parts of Idaho and Wyoming, and what is today Yellowstone Park to within sight

---

RIGHT: Cyrenius Hall's 1878 portrait of Chief Joseph is on display at the National Portrait Gallery in Washington, D.C.

MISSIONARIES AMONG THE NEZ PERCE

❧

Although settlers had been trying to Christianize the Indians since the Pilgrims landed at Plymouth in the seventeenth century, an interest in Christianity among the Nez Perce first arose in 1825, after Canadian fur traders arranged to have two Spokan and Kutenai Indian youths sent to the Red River Mission School in Canada. Later, three Nez Perce youths also attended the school. As a result, the Nez Perce became increasingly interested in the advantages of formal education for their young men. In 1831, some Nez Perces visited Governor William Clark, the former explorer who helped open up the region with Meriwether Lewis, and requested that teachers be sent to their tribe.

In July 1836, the Presbyterian minister Dr. Marcus Whitman and his wife, Narcissa, accompanied by the Reverend Henry Spalding and his wife, Eliza, hauled a wagon over what would become the Oregon Trail to Fort Vancouver. While Whitman established his mission among the Cayuse Indians, the Spaldings ventured 120 miles (192km) east to Lapwai, "Place of the Butterflies," on the Clearwater River, where their mission grew slowly. Other missionaries followed, became a strong influence in the region, and opened Oregon to heavy emigration by settlers.

In July 1839, Spalding traveled to the village of Tuekakas—who became known as Old Joseph—in the Wallowa Valley. He baptized and conducted a Christian marriage for Old Joseph and his wife, as well as other members of the tribe. Then on April 12, 1840, he baptized Old Joseph's baby Ephraim, who would later inherit his father's name, Joseph.

Spalding drove a wedge into the Nez Perce tribe, dividing them into Christians, who followed his preaching, and "heathens," who maintained their traditional beliefs. And when half of the Cayuse tribe died of measles carried by settlers arriving on the Oregon Trail in 1847, rumors spread that Reverend Whitman was actually poisoning the Indians instead of treating them. The Cayuse chief, Tilokaikt, killed Whitman with a tomahawk. In the ensuing massacre, eleven men, Narcissa Whitman, and two children were killed and forty-seven people were captured, later to be ransomed.

Spalding fled from the massacre to Lapwai. On New Year's Day, 1848, friendly Nez Perce escorted him to Fort Walla Walla, which was outside their territory. The Cayuse War raged from 1847 to 1850, after which the Whitman Massacre ringleaders were hung and the Indians' land was opened to homesteading. Although Protestant missionaries were banned from the region, Indian converts maintained the faith; by 1860, the Christian faction comprised two thirds of the Nez Perce tribe.

LEFT: Nez Perce tepees resembled those of the Plains tribes, from whom the Nez Perce absorbed much of their culture. Numbering less than six thousand, the Nez Perce roamed an area covering some twenty-seven thousand miles in what is present-day western Idaho, southeastern Washington, and northeastern Oregon. The region boasts lush prairies, river valleys, towering mountains, and precipitous canyons.

of Canada. Chief Joseph passed the order that there was to be no scalping. The Nez Perce destroyed no property and killed no peaceful settlers along the way.

In contrast, U.S. soldiers broke into the Indian camp and shot and clubbed to death many Indian women and children while Chief Joseph and his warriors were away. Once, under the flag of truce, the army took Joseph prisoner even though he was there to talk peace. Only after the Nez Perce struck back by capturing an army officer did the soldiers agree to release him.

Finally, in 1877 at Eagle Creek in the Bear Paw Mountains only thirty miles from the Canadian border, Joseph stopped to rest his band. There, the cavalry stormed the Nez Perce camp. A few of the Indians managed to make it to Canada, but many of those who escaped to the north died of cold and hunger. Most, however, were trapped, their escape cut off. When it was over, there were many casualties on both sides.

When Joseph consulted with Looking Glass and White Bird, they still refused to give up. But Joseph said, "Many of our people are out on the hills, naked and freezing. The women are suffering with cold; the children are crying with the chilling dampness of the shelter pits. For myself I do not care. It is for them that I am going to surrender."

Mounting his horse, Chief Joseph rode to the soldiers and delivered the following address: "It is cold and we have no blankets. The little children are freezing to death. I want time to look for my children, to see how many of them I can find. Maybe I shall find them among the dead. Hear me, my chiefs. I am tired; my heart is sick and sad. From where the sun now stands, I will fight no more forever." Then he surrendered.

Instead of being taken to the Lapwai Reservation in Idaho, as they were promised, Chief Joseph's tiny band was taken to Indian Territory in Oklahoma. Once there, many of them caught malaria and died, including all six of Joseph's remaining children. Finally, Joseph and some of his people were sent to a reservation in Washington State. They were forced to march the entire way with no supplies, and they arrived in the dead of winter with no food or money.

Chief Joseph never again fought with the whites. Although he longed for the Wallowa Valley, during his final years he tried to educate his people and help make the best of life on the reservation. He died of a heart attack in 1904 and was buried at Nespelem, Washington, where a monument now stands.

RIGHT: When white squatters threatened his lands in 1897, Chief Joseph traveled to Washington, D.C., to petition President McKinley. He then participated in a parade in New York during the dedication of Grant's tomb. Of Chief Joseph's later years, one missionary wrote, "...he held to his heathenism with all the tenacity with which he had clung to his beloved Wallowa Valley."

LEFT: In 1871, a photograph was taken of Chief Looking Glass, a formidable Nez Perce warrior who, like Joseph, spoke against war with the settlers.

CHAPTER TWELVE

Geronimo

When the earth was made;
When the sky was made;
When my songs were first heard;
The holy mountain was standing toward me with life.

—WHITE MOUNTAIN APACHE

THROUGHOUT THE CIVIL WAR AND UP UNTIL the early 1870s, the Apaches, led by such chiefs as Cochise and Mangas Coloradas, resisted confinement on the reservations set up by the U.S. government. The most elusive of these leaders was Geronimo, a war chief of the Chiricahuas. He and his followers repeatedly frustrated their pursuers by fleeing south out of U.S. territory and crossing the border into Mexico. Few in number, the Apaches were the ultimate guerrilla fighters, and Geronimo was supreme among them. Although he led only twenty warriors in his last campaign, he still managed to run a force of five thousand U.S. troops ragged before he was finally captured.

Geronimo was born around 1829 in the mountains near the Gila River near present-day Clifton, Arizona. He was named Goyahkla, meaning "one who yawns." His family belonged to the Bedonkohe band of Chiricahua Apache, a people who were well adapted to living in a land of extremes in temperature, climate, and terrain. They knew every trail and landmark in a forbidding domain of mesas, precipices, canyons, and deserts. They were also known for their skill and ferocity as warriors. For centuries, they maintained a violent hatred of the Spanish and raided many Mexican settlements, always escaping the power of the Spanish army and disappearing into the mountains.

Goyahkla's mother was Juana; his father was Taklishim, or "the gray one." His grandfather, Mahko, was a famous Bedonkohe chief, and Goyahkla grew up listening to stories about this noted warrior. When Goyahkla was ten, he joined the men in hunting. He was trained for warfare from a very young age. He learned to identify every rock and crevice of the land and participated in mock, and very rough, battles with others his own age. By the time of the Gadsen Purchase in 1853, which brought all Chiricahua lands under control of the U.S. government, Goyahkla had already developed a fearsome reputation. The raiding had in fact become so severe that Mexico had adopted a policy of extermination for Apaches, offering rewards for their scalps.

Following the deaths of his mother, wife, and three children in 1858 at the hands of the Mexicans, Goyahkla participated in a battle known as the Ramos incident. Goyahkla, Cochise, and Coloradas raided two companies of the Mexican cavalry, and during the two hours of ferocious fighting that ensued, Goyahkla greatly increased his reputation as a warrior. Venting his grief, Goyahkla killed a number of troopers, believing them to be the same troopers that killed his family. Each time they charged, the Mexicans called to their patron saint, Geronimo, which is the Spanish translation of Jerome. Following the Apache victory, Goyahkla took the name for his own.

During the following years, Geronimo's reputation grew with each bloody raid on a Mexican settlement. He believed his success was due to a vision he had experienced during which a voice called him four times (four being a sacred number), saying, "No gun can ever kill you. I will take the bullets from the guns of the Mexicans, so they will have nothing but powder."

At first, the Apaches were friendly with the white settlers and the U.S. Army, viewing them as allies against the Mexicans. But in 1861, Sec-

---

LEFT: Geronimo's uncompromising nature posed a terrifying threat to the U.S. government.

ABOVE RIGHT: Of his wife and marriage, Geronimo is reported to have said, "She was a good wife, but she was never strong. We followed the traditions of our fathers and we were happy. Three children came to us—children that played, loitered and worked as I had done."

ond Lieutenant George N. Bascom accused Cochise of kidnapping the young son of a settler. Cochise had no knowledge of the boy, who had in fact been kidnapped by a western Apache Coyotero band. Bascom refused to believe him, and while Cochise escaped being arrested, his family was seized.

When Bascom refused to release his hostages, Cochise attacked the Butterfield stagecoach station. He killed one employee, wounded another, and took a third as hostage. When there was still no response from Bascom, the Apache attacked two more stages. Although nobody was killed in these attacks, the army responded by hanging Cochise's brother, two nephews, and three captive Apache warriors; Cochise then executed his own hostages. For the next ten years, Cochise waged war with the Americans with the aid of Coloradas (until Coloradas was executed by the

ABOVE: Apache warriors were masters at defense strategies that took advantage of the forbidding land on which they lived. Most of the trails they left for their pursuers diverged and disappeared into the rocks.

RIGHT: An Apache warrior could cover more than seventy miles a day on foot, alternating between a walk and a trot. He knew how to quench his thirst by holding a pebble in his mouth and could go without water for several days. He also knew where to find water by digging in seemingly parched rock basins.

ABOVE: On horseback, Geronimo posed with Naiche, the son of Cochise, one of the greatest Apache chiefs. In 1876, Naiche succeeded to the hereditary chieftainship of the Chiricahua, but he never attained the statesmanlike stature of his father. Geronimo's own son stands to the right of Naiche.

OPPOSITE, LEFT: General Crook confiscated Naiche's rifle upon his surrender at Fort Bowie in 1886.

OPPOSITE, CENTER: A photograph of Geronimo and Naiche was snapped just after their surrender at Fort Bowie.

OPPOSITE, RIGHT: Geronimo's cavalry carbine was also surrendered at Fort Bowie.

Americans in 1863). At the same time, the government was trying to retire the Apaches to reservations. Resistance to this relocation was at the heart of the Apache rebellion.

The U.S. government finally succeeded in getting Geronimo and the other rebelling groups onto a reservation in San Carlos, Arizona, in 1877. This peace was temporary, however; there was another outbreak of violence in 1881, and although they were not responsible, Geronimo and his followers fled for their lives. They crossed the Mexican border, fighting off the cavalry as they went.

Geronimo was eventually returned to San Carlos, but he didn't stay for long. One night in 1884, Geronimo and other Chiricahua leaders had a long drinking session. They drank *tizwin*, a beer made of crushed and fermented corn. Still under the influence, they confronted a cavalry officer,

demanding the suspension of laws against drinking and wife beating. During the next few days, the Apache people grew nervous and fearful of being arrested and fled from the reservation. Geronimo had apparently instigated the outbreak by telling his fellow Chiricahua leader, Chihuahua, as well as Naiche, Cochise's son and hereditary chieftain of the Chiricahua, that he had killed some cavalrymen. When Naiche found out about Geronimo's lie, he threatened to murder him. As the feuding bands scattered, Chihuahua's band fled to Mexico and killed seventeen civilians along the way. The newspapers blamed Geronimo, whose legend they had helped to create.

Despite their feuding, the Chiricahua bands met up in the Sierra Madre, where Geronimo assumed leadership. They began to raid in even smaller groups until the cavalry, led by traitorous Apaches, attacked

THE INDIAN REORGANIZATION ACT OF 1934

IN 1887, THE ALLOTMENT ACT BECAME LAW, AND THE INDIANS were forced to surrender their reservations. More than one hundred reservations were affected, principally those on the Great Plains, along the Pacific Coast, and in the Great Lakes states. Fragments of reservation land were allotted to individual Indians as small, family-size farms, while the immense "surplus" of remaining land was then made available for purchase by whites. This act broke up tribes, and by one means or another, many allottees also lost their land to white ownership. By the 1920s, Indian poverty was a chronic problem, with the Lakota in South Dakota being hit the hardest. As the Indian population grew over the years, overcrowding on the remaining reservations became an acute problem.

A government-sponsored survey carried out in the late 1920s revealed the incredible economic, educational, and social poverty that most Indians endured. As a result, governmental policies were reversed in the Indian Reorganization Act of 1934, which ended the allotting of tribal lands and tried to reclaim for the Indians the reservation land that had not been homesteaded. The law encouraged a tribal approach to solving Indian problems. Government representatives talked with more than 250 bands and tribes, urging them to organize with constitutions and charters of incorporation and offering loans from a revolving-credit program. Existing bans were lifted on Indian ceremonials and the wearing of Indian dress was encouraged, reawakening a sense of dignity and self-respect in Native Americans.

Geronimo's camp and captured a third of the women and children. Demoralized by the betrayal by their fellow Apaches and exhausted from the cavalry's pursuit, the renegades surrendered on the condition that their exile to the east last not more than two years and that their families be permitted to join them. Geronimo said, "What the others say, I say also. I give myself up to you. Do with me what you please. I surrender. Once I moved about like the wind. Now I surrender to you and that is all."

But it wasn't over yet. Three nights later, drunk on mescal liquor purchased from a trader who told them they were going to be hanged, Geronimo, Naiche, and twenty warriors fled into the rain. They went raiding in Mexico again and killed fourteen settlers during this campaign. Finally, Geronimo surrendered for the last time.

LEFT: Geronimo grew old on the reservation in Oklahoma, where infant mortality remained high. After the death of his own grandson, the elderly Geronimo organized a ceremony to find out if an old man was "witching" the children—killing them—to prolong his own life. Reportedly, the presiding shaman accused Geronimo of being the perpetrator of the evil.

He was sent to Old Fort Pickens, Florida, where he was denied the promised reunion with his family for two years. He became a popular tourist attraction until 1894, when he was removed to Fort Sill, Indian Territory, in the present state of Oklahoma. There, the Apaches were divided into villages, each under a headman. Geronimo served as the leader of a village, receiving an army uniform and the pay of an army scout. The Apaches farmed and raised cattle, but their death rate was mysteriously high. Geronimo attributed this to being taken away from their sacred homeland.

Geronimo was "exhibited" in a Cadillac at Theodore Roosevelt's inauguration in 1901, and he received excellent appearance fees. He also earned a considerable amount of money, which he invested, by manufacturing bows and arrows at Fort Sill.

Geronimo's preference for alcohol continued throughout the later years of his life, and in February 1909, when he was in his eighties, he fell drunk from his horse and spent the night sprawled in damp weeds. He contracted pneumonia and died. Geronimo, a symbol of Indian resistance, the last renegade, and the most determined foe of the U.S. government, was gone.

Twentieth-Century Chiefs

MATTHEW KING, LAKOTA CHIEF

Matthew King was a well-known traditionalist Lakota spokesman and spiritual leader who lived on Pine Ridge Reservation, South Dakota, until his death in 1983. In the book *Wisdomkeepers,* which profiles Native American elders, he spoke for himself. "My Indian name is Noble Red Man," he said. "I'm a chief. I say what I have to say. That's my duty. If I don't say it, who's going to say it for me?"

Like his fathers before him, King made frequent vision quests into the hills for several days and nights without food or water to communicate with the Great Spirit. Once, when he was praying to the Great Spirit for a cure for diabetes, he heard a voice say, "Turn around." When he did, the most beautiful woman he'd ever seen was standing there. She held dark blue berries from a cedar tree in her hand. Then she disappeared.

King knew she was White Buffalo Calf Woman, the one responsible for bringing the sacred pipe to the Lakota. The story goes that long ago the Lakota were starving as punishment for straying from the Great Spirit. No matter where they traveled or where they looked, the hunters could find no game. The Great Spirit sent White Buffalo Calf Woman to save the people. She brought them the pipe so that they could pray and talk with the Great Spirit whenever they wanted.

"I knew when I saw her up on the mountain that this was the same woman," King said. But she disappeared before he could take the berries from her. He forgot about them, and years later when he got diabetes, he went to the white men's doctors. They gave him insulin. "Then I remembered White Buffalo Calf Woman and those little blue cedar berries," he said. "I picked some, boiled them, strained the juice, and drank it. It's so bitter it took the sugar right out of my body. The doctors checked me and were amazed. They said the diabetes was gone."

King was also the keeper of Red Cloud's peace pipe. Although he held his warrior ancestors in the highest regard, King saw peace as the method for solving problems. "The peace pipe is our only weapon," he said. "It's our holy power. It's the Great Spirit's power. The pipe mediates between man and God."

Before his death, King prophesied the Great Spirit's judgment on the world. He believed that every living thing on earth was going to perish and that it would be another million years before life began again. "Grandmother Earth will be alone," he said. "She's going to rest. All because of the white man's wickedness."

King pointed to the Mount St. Helens volcanic eruption as a sign. "And there's going to be earthquakes; maybe half of California and half of Washington and Oregon will go into the water," he said. "The same in the East and in the South. You're going to have volcanoes and earthquakes and hurricanes.

"You are going to learn the most important lesson—that God is the most powerful thing there is.... Maybe you can change, maybe you can stop what's coming. There's not much time. It's going to happen. Take it from me. Tell them Noble Red Man said so!"

OREN LYONS, ONONDAGA CHIEF

Oren Lyons lives on the Onondaga reservation a few miles south of Syracuse, New York, in a house with no electricity and no phones, which is his preference. Lyons is a Faithkeeper of the Turtle Clan of the Onondaga Nation and a spokesman for the Six Nations Iroquois Confederacy, which is based on the organization formed by Hiawatha and Deganawidah (the Peacemaker) in the sixteenth century.

Orens is also a political activist who is concerned with environmental issues. He perceives the laws of human beings as being in conflict with natural law. For example, while human life depends on the existence of pure water, laws are passed that condone dumping of waste into rivers and lakes. "If you kill the water, you kill the life that depends on it, your own included," he believes. "That's natural law. It's also common sense."

In their commonsense way of life and in their governmental decision-making processes, the Iroquois are forward-looking and consider the next generation of their people, which is known as the Seventh Generation, when they plan for the future. Their government makes decisions for the tribes during highly structured council meetings of the confederacy. Each of the Six Nations comes together as equals around a three-sided council fire. The Onondaga's Elder Brothers, the Seneca and Mohawk, sit on one side; their Younger Brothers, the Oneida, Cayuga, and Tuscadora, sit on the other side. In front sit the Onondaga, the keepers of the Central Fire. Each side of the fire has one speaker, who talks on behalf of those with whom he sits.

A problem is presented from what is known as "the Well." Then, each side has an opportunity for discussion and sends their decision on the problem back to the Well. There the solutions are adjusted to conform with the decisions of the other sides, and the problem is sent back out from the Well again. This process continues until the issue is unanimously decided.

This method of decision-making is time-consuming, but once a decision is reached, it is very firm. "The Peacemaker who founded our Confederacy told us, we must be of one mind," Lyons says. "Those are good words to remember today—or any day."

WILMA MANKILLER, CHEROKEE CHIEF

Wilma Mankiller was born in Stilwell, Oklahoma, in 1945. In 1987, she was elected the first female chief of the 108,000-member Cherokee Nation, the second-largest tribe in the United States after the Navajos. Mankiller, who inherited her last name from an eighteenth-century warrior ancestor, attended college in California before returning to Oklahoma. Prior to her 1987 election to principal chief, she served as both community development director and deputy chief. She has likened her current job to "running a small country, a medium-size corporation, and being a social worker." The tribe operates industries, health clinics, and cultural programs employing several thousand people.

Mankiller believes that Native Americans must look within their own history, culture, and value systems for solutions to their problems. She identifies self-determination as being at the heart of this issue, noting the difference between the U.S. government's view of self-government and that of native peoples. "The federal law's idea of self-determination is that the U.S. government still wants to hold our hands and tell us what we can and can't do," she says.

Mankiller acknowledges the difficulty of preserving traditional values as the Cherokee Nation becomes a modern economic entity. During her father's time, it was believed that there were only two options. The first was to remain a traditional Cherokee and not interact with larger society at all. "In fact, one of my uncles thought you were totally lost if you went to school past the eighth grade because you became enculturated," she recalls. The other option was to give up your heritage completely in order to make it in the world.

But times have changed. Mankiller encourages her people to see that Cherokees have a set of values that they can take wherever they go. She sees this as the most important factor in retaining Cherokee culture. While she knows some of her fellow tribes people would disagree, she believes that such things as dressing appropriately for a traditional ceremony have less to do with retaining the culture than with maintaining a traditional value system.

Mankiller does appreciate some of what contemporary rock and pop culture has to offer Cherokee youth. In particular, she appreciates rap music. "I lived in a predominantly black housing project during my youth in San Francisco," she says. "Rap is a nice reflection of a culture that wouldn't be heard otherwise." She views listening to rap as a way to expose rural Cherokee youth to urban culture.

Protecting indigenous culture, including the teaching of the Cherokee language in schools, is one of Mankiller's goals as principal chief. Software programs of the Cherokee written language are being used in even the most rural schools where children work with computers. "We hope to be able to adapt that in some way to teach reading to those who speak Cherokee," she says. "And to teach Cherokee to the people who don't already know it."

Mankiller does not believe that the educational system in the United States adequately addresses the history and contributions of Native Americans. She attributes this to people simply not wanting to deal with the truth. "No one wants to hear about the San Creek Massacre, the Trail of Tears, the incredible brutality toward the California Indians, or the Wounded Knee Massacre," she says. "They want us to be invisible so they can hang onto their myths about the brave frontier families."

Participating in traditional ceremonial practices is another way of protecting Cherokee culture, according to Mankiller. "I always try to mention to people who think I am a postmodern Indian, that I use a traditional medicine man, and that medicine people and traditional healing practices existed long before Harvard medical school."

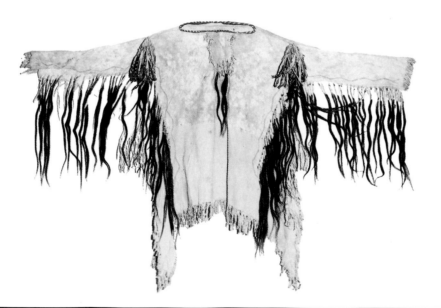

Native American Organizations

ARIZONA

National Native American
    Cooperative
P.O. Box 5000
San Carlos, AZ 85550-0301
(602) 230-3399

United Indian Missions
    International
P.O. Box 3600
Flagstaff, AZ 86003-3600
(602) 774-0651

CALIFORNIA

American Indian Movement
710 Clayton Street, Apt. 1
San Francisco, CA 94117
(415) 566-0251

United Native Americans
2434 Faria Avenue
Pinole, CA 94564
(415) 758-8160

COLORADO

National Urban Indian Council
10555 Jewell Avenue
Denver, CO 80226
(303) 985-5260

CONNECTICUT

American Indian Archaeology
    Institute
Curtis Road
P.O. Box 1260
Washington, CT 06793-0260
(203) 868-0518

Save the Children Foundation
54 Wilton Road
Westport, CT 06880
(203) 221-1260

DISTRICT OF COLUMBIA

Arrow, Inc.
1000 Connecticut Avenue,
    N.W., Suite 1206
Washington, DC 20036
(202) 296-0685

National Congress of American
    Indians
900 Pennsylvania Avenue, S.E.
Washington, DC 20036
(202) 546-9404

ILLINOIS

Native American Program
Commission for Multicultural
    Ministries of ELCA
8765 West Higgens Road
Chicago, IL 60631
(312) 380-2838

IOWA

Indian Youth of America
609 Badgerow Building
P.O. Box 2786
Souix City, IA 51106
(712) 252-3230

MICHIGAN

North American Indian
    Association
22720 Plymouth Road
Detroit, MI 48239
(313) 535-2966

NEW MEXICO

Gathering of Nations
P.O. Box 75102, Sta. 14
Albuquerque, NM 87194
(505) 836-2810

Indian Youth Council
318 Elm Street, S.E.
Albuquerque, NM 87102
(505) 247-2251

Inter-Tribal Indian Ceremonial
    Association
Box 1
Church Rock, NM 87311
(505) 863-3896

NEW YORK

Association on American Indian
    Affairs
95 Madison Avenue
New York, NY 10016
(212) 689-8720

Council for Native American
    Indians
280 Broadway, Suite 316
New York, NY 10007
(212) 732-0485

OHIO

American Indian Lore Association
960 Walhonding Avenue
Logan, OH 43138
(614) 385-7136

OKLAHOMA

Association of American Indian
    Physicians
Building D
10015 S. Pennsylvania
Oklahoma City, OK 73159
(405) 692-1202

Cherokee National Historical
    Society
P.O. Box 515
Tahlequah, OK 74465
(918) 456-6007

Creek Indian Memorial
    Association
Creek County House Museum
Town Square
Okmulgee, OK 74447
(918) 756-2324

OREGON

Institute for the Study of
    Traditional American Indian
    Arts
P.O. Box 66124
Portland, OR 97266
(505) 863-3896

PENNSYLVANIA

American Friends Service
    Committee
1501 Cherry Street
Philadelphia, PA 19102
(215) 241-7000

Indian Rights Association
c/o Janney Montgomery
1601 Market Street
Philadelphia, PA 19103
(215) 665-4523

SOUTH DAKOTA

Native American Community
    Board
P.O. Box 572
Lake Andes, SD 57356-0572
(605) 487-7072

North American Indian Women's
    Association
P.O. Box 805
Eagle Butte, SD 57625
(605) 964-2136

TENNESSEE

United South and Eastern Tribes
1101 Kermit Drive, Suite 800
Nashville, TN 37217

VIRGINIA

American Indian Heritage
    Foundation
6051 Arlington Boulevard
Falls Church, VA 22044
(202) IND-IANS

WASHINGTON

Survival of American Indian
    Association
7803-A Samurai Drive, S.E.
Olympia, WA 98503

United Indians of All Tribes
    Foundation
Daybreak Star Arts Center
Discovery Park
P.O. Box 99100
Seattle, WA 98199
(206) 285-4425

Native American Museums

ALABAMA

Birmingham Museum of Art
2000 8th Avenue N.
Birmingham, AL 35203
(205) 254-2566

ARIZONA

The Heard Museum
22 E. Monte Vista
Phoenix, AZ 85004
(602) 252-8840

Pueblo Grande Museum and
    Cultural Park
4619 E. Washington
Phoenix, AZ 85034
(602) 495-0901

Tusayan Museum
Yavapai Museum
Grand Canyon National Park
Box 129
Grand Canyon, AZ 86023
(602) 638-7797

ARKANSAS

Desha County Museum
Highway 165
Dumas, AR 71639
(501) 382-4222

Ka-Do-Ha Discovery Museum
P.O. Box 669
Murfreesboro, AR 71958
(501) 285-3736

CALIFORNIA

Cabot's Old Indian Pueblo
    Museum
67-616 Desert View Avenue
Desert Hot Springs, CA 92240
(619) 329-7610

Southwest Museum
234 Museum Drive
Los Angeles, CA 90065
(213) 221-2164

State Indian Museum
2618 K Street
Sacramento, CA 95816
(916) 324-0971

COLORADO

Koshare Indian Museum, Inc.
115 West 18th
La Junta, CO 81050
(719) 385-4411

Natural History Museum
City Park
Denver, CO 80205
(303) 370-6357

Ute Indian Museum
17253 Chipeta Drive
Montrose, CO 81401

CONNECTICUT

Tantaquidgeon Indian Museum
Route 32 Norwich-New
    London Road
Montville, CT 06382
(203) 848-9145

DELAWARE

Lewes Historical Society
110 Shipcarpenter Street
Lewes, DE 19958
(302) 645-7670

DISTRICT OF COLUMBIA

Indian Arts and Crafts Board
18th and C Streets, N.W.,
    Room 4004-MIB
Washington, DC 20240
(202) 208-3773

United States Department of
    the Interior Museum
1849 C Street, N.W.
Washington, DC 20240
(202) 208-4743

FLORIDA

Florida Community College,
    Kent Campus Museum
    Gallery
3939 Roosevelt Boulevard
Jacksonville, FL 32205
(904) 387-8374

GEORGIA

Etowah Indian Mounds Historical
 Site
813 Indian Mounds Road, S.W.
Cartersville, GA 30120
(706) 387-3747

Indian Springs State Park Museum
Indian Springs State Park
Indian Springs, GA 30216
(706) 775-7241

Vann House
GA 225 & Alt. GA 527
Spring Place, GA 30705
(706) 695-2598

IDAHO

Massacre Rocks State Park
3592 N. Park Lane
American Falls, ID 83211
(208) 548-2672

Nez Perce National Historical Park
Highway 95
Spalding, ID 83551
(208) 843-2261

ILLINOIS

Cahokia Mounds State Historic
 Site
30 Ramey Street
East Saint Louis, IL 62201
(618) 346-5160

Field Museum of Natural History
Lake Shore Drive and Roosevelt
 Road
Chicago, IL 60605
(312) 922-9410

INDIANA

Eiteljorg Museum of American
 Indian and Western Art
500 W. Washington
Indianapolis, IN 46204
(317) 636-9378

Monroe County Historical Society
 Museum
202 E. Sixth Street
Bloomington, IN 47401
(812) 332-2517

IOWA

Effigy Mounds National
 Monument
RR 1, Box 25 A
Harpers Ferry, IA
(319) 873-3491

KANSAS

Last Indian Raid Museum
258 S. Penn Avenue
Oberlin, KS 67749
(913) 475-2712

Pawnee Indian Village Museum
Route 1, Box 475
Republic, KS 66964
(913) 361-2255

Kansas Museum of History
6425 S.W. Sixth Street
Topeka, KS 66615-1099
(913) 272-8681

KENTUCKY

Museum of Anthropology
211 Lafferty Hall
University of Kentucky
Lexington, KY 40506-0024
(606) 257-7112

LOUISIANA

Lafayette Natural History Museum
637 Girard Park Drive
Lafayette, LA 70503
(318) 268-5544

MAINE

Maine Tribal Unity Museum
Quaker Hill Road
Unity, ME 04988
(207) 948-3131

MARYLAND

Fort Frederick State Park
11100 Fort Frederick Road
Big Pool, MD 21711
(301) 842-2155

MASSACHUSETTS

Peabody Museum of Archaeology
 and Ethnology
11 Divinity Avenue
Cambridge, MA 02138
(617) 495-2248

MICHIGAN

Andrew J. Blackbird Museum
368 E. Main Street
Harbor Springs, MI 49740
(616) 526-7731

University of Michigan Museum
 of Anthropology
4009 Ruthven Museums Building
Ann Arbor, MI 48109
(313) 764-6485

Wayne State University Museum
 of Anthropology
6001 Cass Avenue
Detroit, MI 48202
(313) 577-2598

MINNESOTA

Minnesota Historical Society
690 Cedar Street
St. Paul, MN 55101
(612) 296-6126

Pipestone National Monument
P.O. Box 727
Pipestone, MN 56164
(507) 825-5464

MISSOURI

St. Louis Science Center
5050 Oakland Avenue
St. Louis, MO 63110
(314) 289-4400

University of Missouri Museum of
 Anthropology
104 Swallow Hall
Columbia, MO 65211
(314) 882-3764

Van Meter State Park
Route 122
Miami, MO 65344
(816) 886-7537

MONTANA

Museum of Plains Indians and
    Crafts Center
U.S. Highway 8922
Browning, MT 59417
(406) 338-2230

NEBRASKA

Museum of the Fur Trade
East Highway 20
Chadron, NE 69337
(308) 432-3843

NEVADA

Nevada Historical Society
1650 N. Virginia Street
Reno, NV 89503
(702) 688-1190

NEW HAMPSHIRE

Old Fort Number 4 Associates
Springfield Road, Route 11
Charlestown, NH 03603
(605) 826-5700

NEW JERSEY

Lake Hopatcong Historical
    Museum
Lake Hopatcong State Park
Landing, NJ 07850
(201) 398-2616

NEW MEXICO

Aztec Ruins National Monument
Ruins Road
Aztec, NM 87410
(505) 334-6174

Institute of American Indian Arts
    Museum
1369 Cerillos Road
Santa Fe, NM 87504
(505) 988-6281

Maxwell Museum of
    Anthropology
University and Ash N.E.
Albuquerque, NM 87131-1202
(505) 277-4404

Wheelwright Museum of the
    American Indian
704 Camino Lejo
Santa Fe, NM 87501
(505) 982-4636

NEW YORK

American Museum of Natural
    History
Central Park West and 79th Street
New York, NY 10024
(212) 769-5000

Brooklyn Museum
200 Eastern Parkway
Brooklyn, NY 11238
(718) 638-5000

Fort Plain Museum
Canal Street
Fort Plain, NY 13339
(518) 993-2527

Metropolitan Museum of Art
Fifth Avenue at 82nd Street
New York, NY 10028
(212) 879-5500

The Mohawk-Caughnawaga
    Museum
Route 5
Fonda, NY 12068
(518) 853-3646

Museum of the American Indian,
    Smithsonian Institution
Broadway and 155th Street
New York, NY 10032-1596
(212) 283-2420

Six Nations Museum
Roakdale Road, HCR#1 Box 10
Onchiota, NY 12968
(518) 891-0769

NORTH CAROLINA

Museum of the Cherokee Indian
U.S. 441
Cherokee, NC 28719
(704) 497-3481

NORTH DAKOTA

Fort Abraham Lincoln State
    Historical Park
Route 2 Box 139
Mandan, ND 58554
(701) 663-9571

Turtle Mountain Chippewa
    Heritage Center
Highway 5, P.O. Box 257
Belcourt, ND 58316
(701) 477-6140

OHIO

Ohio Historical Center
Interstate 71 and 17th Avenue
Columbus, OH 43211
(614) 297-2300

OKLAHOMA

Cherokee National Museum
TSA-LA-GI-Cherokee Heritage
    Center
Willis Road
Tahlequah, OK 74465
(918) 456-6007

Creek Council House Museum
Town Square
Okmulgee, OK 74447
(918) 756-2324

The Five Civilized Tribes Museum
Agency Hill
Honor Heights Drive
Muskogee, OK 74401

Memorial Indian Museum
Second and Allen Streets
Broken Bow, OK 74728
(405) 584-6531

National Hall of Fame for Famous
    American Indians
Highway 62
Anadarko, OK 73005
(405) 247-5555

Oklahoma Historical Society
2100 North Lincoln Boulevard
Oklahoma City, OK 73105
(405) 521-2491

Ponca City Cultural Center
 Museum
1000 East Grand
Ponca City, OK 74601
(405) 767-0427

Sequoyah's Home
Route 1, Box 141
Sallisaw, OK 74955
(918) 775-2413

Southern Plains Indian Museum
 and Crafts Center
P.O. Box 749
Highway 62, East
Anadarko, OK 73005
(405) 247-6221

OREGON

Portland Art Museum
1219 S.W. Park Avenue
Portland, OR 97205
(503) 226-2811

PENNSYLVANIA

The University Museum of
 Archaeology and
 Anthropology, University of
 Pennsylvania
33rd and Spruce Streets
Philadelphia, PA 19104-6324
(215) 898-4000

RHODE ISLAND

Haffenreffer Museum of
 Anthropology, Brown Museum
Mt. Hope Grant
Bristol, RI 02809
(401) 253-8388

SOUTH CAROLINA

Beaufort Museum
713 Cravens Street
Beaufort, SC 29901
(803) 525-7471

SOUTH DAKOTA

American Indian Culture Research
 Center
Blue Cloud Abbey
P.O. Box 98
Marvin, SD 57251
(605) 432-5528

The Heritage Center, Inc.
Mari Sandoz Museum
Red Cloud Indian School
Pine Ridge, SD 57770
(605) 867-5491

Sioux Indian Museum and Crafts
 Center
515 West Boulevard
Rapid City, SD 57701
(605) 348-0557

TENNESSEE

Shiloh National Military Park and
 Cemetery
Highway 22
Shiloh, TN 38376
(901) 689-5275

TEXAS

Caddo Indian Museum
701 Hardy Street
Longview, TX 75604
(903) 759-5739

Texas Memorial Museum
2400 Trinity
Austin, TX 78705
(512) 471-1604

UTAH

Utah Museum of Natural History
University of Utah
Salt Lake City, UT 84112
(801) 581-6927

VERMONT

Vermont Museum
109 State Street, Pavilion Building
Montpelier, VT 05609-0901
(802) 828-2291

VIRGINIA

Fredericksburg Area Museum and
 Cultural Center
907-911 Princess Anne Street
Fredericksburg, VA 22401
(703) 371-5668

WASHINGTON

Thomas Burke Memorial
 Washington State Museum
University of Washington Campus
Seattle, WA 98195
(206) 543-5590

WEST VIRGINIA

Delf Norona Museum and
 Cultural Center
801 Jefferson Avenue
Moundsville, WV 26041
(304) 843-1410

WISCONSIN

Logan Museum of Anthropology
Prospect and Bushnell
Beloit, WI 53511
(608) 363-2677

Milwaukee Public Museum
800 West Wells Street
Milwaukee, WI 53233
(414) 278-2702

WYOMING

Fort Casper Museum
4001 Fort Casper Road
Casper, WY 82601
(307) 235-8462

Plains Indians Museum
Buffalo Bill Historical Center
720 Sheridan Avenue
Cody, WY 82414
(307) 587-4771

Wyoming State Museum
Barret Building
2301 Central Avenue
Cheyenne, WY 82001
(307) 777-7022

•BIBLIOGRAPHY•

Bierhorst, John, ed. *The Sacred Path: Spells, Prayers & Power Songs of the American Indians.* New York: William Morrow and Company, 1983.

Brown, Dee. *Bury My Heart at Wounded Knee.* New York: Holt, Rinehart and Winston, 1970.

Browne, Jackson. "Cherokee Nation." New York: *Spin* magazine, November 1991.

Harris, Marvin. *Cows, Pigs, Wars and Witches: The Riddles of Culture.* New York: Vintage Books/Random House, 1974.

Hauck, Philomena, and Kathleen M. Snow. *Following Historic Trails: Famous Indian Leaders.* Calgary, Alberta: Detselig Enterprises Limited, 1989.

Hook, Jason. *American Indian Warrior Chiefs.* United Kingdom: Firebird Books, 1989.

Hungry Wolf, Adolf, and Beverly Hungry Wolf. *Indian Tribes of the Northern Rockies.* Skookumchuck, B.C.: Good Medicine Books, 1989.

Josephy, Jr., Alvin M. *The Patriot Chiefs: A Chronicle of American Indian Resistance.* New York: Viking, 1961.

_____. *The American Heritage Book of Indians.* New York: American Heritage Publishing Company, 1961.

LaFarge, Oliver. *A Pictorial History of the American Indian.* New York: Crown Publishers, 1956.

Neihardt, John G. (Flaming Rainbow). *Black Elk Speaks.* Lincoln, Nebr.: Bison Books/University of Nebraska Press, 1961.

Wall, Steve, and Harvey Arden. *Wisdomkeepers.* Hillsboro, Oreg.: Beyond Words Publishing, Inc., 1990.

White, Jon Manchip. *Everyday Life of the North American Indians.* New York: Dorset Press, 1979.

Woodcock, George. *Peoples of the Coast: The Indians of the Pacific Northwest.* Bloomington, Ind.: Indiana University Press, 1977.

•INDEX•

Alaska, 40, 41
Alcohol, 48, 51, 60, 99
Alligator, 54, 57
Allotment Act, 99
American Horse, *78*, 83
Amherst, Sir Jeffrey, 31, 35
Apache tribe, 92, 93, 94, 97, 99
Arapaho tribe, 64, 66
Arizona, 24, 28, 92
Assembly of First Nations, 42, 43
Athapascan tribe, 42
Atotarho, 11, 12, 13
Awashonks, 17, 18, 21

Bascom, George, *93*
Bat, 80
Battle of the Thames, 51
Beaver tribe, 42
Big Horse Steal, 74
Blackfoot tribe, 42, *43*
Black Hawk, 58–63, *58*
Black Kettle, 79
Blood feud, 11, 13
Blue Jacket, 48
Bozeman Trail, 83
Bua, Nicolas, 28
Buffalo, 64, 70, 74, 84
Buffalo Bill. *See* Cody, Buffalo Bill.

California, 40
Cannibalism, 12, 13
Canonchet, 18, 21
Carrier tribe, 42
Catlin, George, 57, 58, 61
Cayse tribe, 89

Cayuga tribe, 11, 101
Ceremonies, 25, 102
    religious, 25
Charlo, 86
Cheesekau, 47
Cherokee tribe, 48, 57, 101, 102
Cheyenne tribe, 64, 66, 70, 75, 78,
    79, 80
Chickasaw tribe, 57
Chiefs, 13
    Alligator, 54, 57
    American Horse, *78*, 83
    Awashonks, 17, 18, 21
    Bat, 80
    Big Foot, *72*
    Black Hawk, 58–63, *58*
    Black Kettle, 79
    Blue Jacket, 48
    Callicum, 39
    Canonchet, 18, 21
    Cochise, 92, 93
    Coloradas, 92, 93
    Conquering Bear, 75
    Crazy Horse, 66, 74–83, *83*
    Four Winds, 66
    Geronimo, 92–99, *92, 96, 97, 98*
    Joseph, 84–91, *87, 91*
    Keokuk, 58–63
    Loud-Voiced Hawk, 66
    Maquinna, 36–45, *36*
    Matoonas, 18, 21
    Michikinikwa, 47
    Monoco, 18
    One-Eyed John, 18
    Philip, 16–23

Pontiac, 30–35, *30*
Red Cloud, 67, 80, 83, 100
Red Horn, 66
Running Antelope, 66
Shoshanim, 18, 21
Sitting Bull, 79
Tecumseh, 46–51, 53
Wild Cat, 54, 57
Chinook tribe, 40
Chippewa tribe, 10, 30, 31, *32*,
    35, 47
Chiricahua tribe, 92, 96, 97
Chocktaw tribe, 57
Christianity, 24, 37, 85, 89
Church, Benjamin, 18, 21, 22
Clark, William, 85, 89
Cochise, 92, 93
Cody, Buffalo Bill, *70*, 71
Coloradas, 92, 93
Conestoga tribe, 11
Connecticut, 17, 18, 21
Cook, Captain James, 37
Corn Dance, 10
Counting coup, 64, 65
Crazy Horse, 74–83, *83*
Creek tribe, 46, 52, 53, 57
Creek War, 53
Cree tribe, 42, *42*, 43
Crow tribe, 64, 75, 80
Custer, General George, 64, 65,
    70, 71, 74, 80, 83

Deganawidah, 13, 14, 101
Delaware tribe, 31, 35, 48, 51
Djigosasee, 14

Dog-rib tribe, 42

Erie tribe, 11
Eskimos, 42

Five Nations, 10, 12, 13, *14*
Five Wounds, 86
Florida, 54, 57
Forts
    Buford, 70
    de Chartres, 35
    Detroit, 31, 32
    Laramie, 80
    Miami, 35
    Pitt, 35, 47
    St. Joseph, 35
    Sandusky, 35
    Sill, 99
    Vancouver, 89
Fox tribe, 31, 58, 59, 60
French and Indian war, 35
Fur trading, 30–31

Gadsden Purchase, 93
Galloway, Rebecca, 48
Geronimo, 92–99, *92, 96, 97, 98*
Ghost Dance, 71
Gladwin, Major Henry, 35
Great Peace, 10, 12, 13, 15
Great Spirit, 65, 66, 70, 100
Greenville Treaty, 46, 47, 48
Grizzly Bear Ferocious, 86

Harrison, General William Henry,
    48, 49

Hiawatha, 10–14, *10–11*, *13*, 101
Honnaisont tribe, 11
Hopis, *27*, *28*
Howard, General O. O., 86
Hunkpapa tribe, 64, 72
Hunkpatila tribe, 74
Hunt, Thomas, 16
Hupa tribe, 40
Huron tribe, 11, 14, 31, 32, 35

Illinois, 31, 35, 58
Indiana, 31, 47
Indian Reorganization Act, 99
Indian Territory, 53, 54, 57, 90, 99
Indian Wars, 47, 58
Iroquois tribe, 10, 11, 12, 13, 14
Irrigation, 28

Joseph, *87*, *91*
Jumping Bull, 65, 71

Karok tribe, 40
Keokuk, 58–63
Kickapoo tribe, 31, 49
King, Matthew, 100–101
Kivas, 25, *25*

Lakota tribe, 64, 65, 67, 70, 74, 75, 80, 83, 99, 100–101
Lewis, Meriwether, 85, 89
Little Bighorn, 64
Little Big Man, *82*, 83
Longfellow, Henry Wadsworth, 10
Looking Glass, 86, 90, *90*
Lyons, Oren, 101

Mackay, John, 37
Maine, 15
Mankiller, Wilma, 101–102
Maquinna, 36–45, *36*
Mascouten tribe, 31
Massachusetts, 16, 21
Massasoit, 16, 17, *17*
Master of Life, 11, 13, 14, 31, 51
Mather, Cotton, 21
Matoonas, 18, 21
Mattaump, 18
Medicine men, 10, 24, 25, 28, 66, 102
Menominee tribe, 31
Mercredi, Ovide, 43
Metacom, 17
Methoataske, 46

Miami tribe, 30–35, 47
Michikinikwa, 47
Mingo tribe, 35
Minneconjou tribe, 72
Mississippi, 57
Missouri, 47, 58, 60, 83
Mohawk tribe, 10, 11, 13, 101
Mohegan tribe, 17, 18, 21
Monoco, 18
Montana, 80, 83, 86

Narraganset tribe, 17, 18, 21
Navajo tribe, 101
Neolin, 31, 51
New Mexico, 24, 25, 28
New York, 10, 11, 13, 15, 101
Nez Perce tribe, 84, 85, *85*, 86, 89, 90
Niantic tribe, 17, 21
Nipmuck tribe, 17, 18, 21
Noble Red Man, 100
Nootka tribe, 36, 37, 40
North Dakota, 70

Oakley, Annie, 70
Oglala tribe, 78, 80, 83
Ohio, 11, 31, 46, 47
Ohwachiras, 13, 14
Oklahoma, 51, 53, 54, 57, 62, 90, 99, 101
One-eyed John, 18
Oneida tribe, 11, 13, 101
Onondaga tribe, 10, 11, 12, 101
Oregon Trail, 69, 75
Orenda, 14
Osage tribe, 59
Osceola, 52–57, *52*
Ottawa tribe, 31, 35, 49

Pawnee tribe, 75, 80
Pennsylvania, 11, 31, 35
Peoria tribe, 35
Pequot tribe, 17, 21
Persecution of Indians, 17, 21, 22, 30, 31, 35, 60, 75, 80, 86, 89
Philip, King, 16–23, *16*, *20*
Piankashaw tribe, 31
Pilgrims, 16, 17, *17*
Plymouth Colony, 16, 21, 22
Pocasset tribe, 18
Pontiac, 30–35, *30*
Popé, 24–29
Potawatomi tribe, 31, 32, 35, 47, 49

Potlatch, 44, 45
Powell, Billy. *See* Osceola.
Prophet's Town, 48, 49
Pueblo tribe, 24–29

Railroads, 67, 70
Rainbow, 86
Red Cloud, 80, 83, *83*, 100
Red Owl, 86
Removal Bill, 57
Reservations, 42, 64, 67, 70, 71, 72, 83, 86, 90, 97, 99, 100, 101
Rhode Island, 17, 21

Sachems. *See* Chiefs.
Sakonnet tribe, 17, 18
Salish tribe, 37, 40
Sand Creek Massacre, 66, 102
Sauk tribe, 31, 48, 58, 59, 60
Scalping, 59, 93
Seminole tribe, 48, 52, 53, 54, 57
Seminole War, 53, 54
Seneca tribe, 11, 13, 101
Shawnee tribe, 31, 46, 47, 51
Shononi tribe, 80
Shoshanim, 18, 21
Shoshone tribe, 64, 75
Sioux tribe, 64, 71, 74
Sitting Bull, 64–73, *64*, *70*, *71*, *73*, 74, 79
Six Songs, 13
Slavery, 16, 40, 53, 57
Slave tribe, 42
Small Grizzly Bear Claw. *See* Charlo.
Snake tribe, 64
South Dakota, 64, 99, 100
Spalding, Rev. Henry, 89
Spirits, 25, 28
Spotted Tail, 83
Sully, General Alfred, 77
Sun Dance, 66, 67, 70, 75
Susquehannock tribe, 11
Sword, 83

Tallassee tribe, 52, 53
Taos pueblo, *27*
Taylor, Zachary, 54
Tecumseh, 46–51, *46*, 53
Tee Yee Neen Ho Ga Row, *13*
Teharonhiawagon, 11
Tennessee, 15
Tenskwatawa, 48, 49, 51, *51*

Teton tribe, 64, 74
Tewa tribe, 24
Thief Treaty, 85
Tieume, 28
Tilini, 28
Tlingit tribe, 40, *40*
Tomahawks, *62*
Toohoolhoolzote, 86
Totem poles, 40, *41*
Trading, fur, 30–31, 37, 40
Traditional beliefs, 24–25
Treaty of 1868, 67, 80
Tuscarora tribe, 13, 15, 101
Tustenuggee, 53

U. S. Army, 60, 63, 70, 78, 84, 86, 89, 90, 93

Vancouver, George, 37
Vancouver Island, 36–45
Vision quest, 65, 66, 75, 100

Wallowa tribe, 86
Wampanoag tribe, 17, 21, 22
Wampum, *11*, 13, 17
Wamsutta, 16
War belts, 32
Warfare
    with British, 32, 35
    colonial, 16, 21, 30–35, 47
    French and Indian war, 35
    intertribal, 11, 12
    with Spaniards, 28
War of 1812, 49, 52–53, 59
Wasamegin, 17
Wayne, "Mad" Anthony, 47
Wea tribe, 31
Weaving, *32*, *37*
Wetamoo, 18, 21
White Bird, 86, 90
Whitman, Dr. Marcus, 89
Wild Cat, 54, 57
Winnebago tribe, 31, 48, 49, 58, 60, *62*
Wisconsin, 31, 58
Wolf dance, 37
Wounded Knee, 72, 83, 102
Wyandot tribe, 49
Wyoming, 83, 86

Yellowknife tribe, 42
Yurok tribe, 40